EYE ON
Art

MANGA

by Stuart A. Kallen

LUCENT BOOKS
A part of Gale, Cengage Learning

GALE
CENGAGE Learning™

Detroit • New York • San Francisco • New Haven, Conn • Waterville, Maine • London

© 2011 Gale, Cengage Learning

LIBRARY OF CONGRESS CATALOGING-IN-PUBLICATION DATA

Kallen, Stuart A., 1955-
 Manga / by Stuart A. Kallen.
    p. cm. -- (Eye on art)
 Includes bibliographical references and index.
 ISBN 978-1-4205-0535-1 (hardcover)
 1. Comic books, strips, etc.--Japan. I. Title.
 NC1764.5.J3K35 2011
 741.5'952--dc22

                                                  2011002418

Lucent Books
27500 Drake Rd.
Farmington Hills, MI 48331

ISBN-13: 978-1-4205-0535-1
ISBN-10: 1-4205-0535-1

Printed in the United States of America
1 2 3 4 5 6 7 15 14 13 12 11

Printed by Bang Printing, Brainerd, MN, 1st Ptg., 05/2011

Contents

Foreword 5

Introduction 8
Whimsical Pictures

Chapter 1 12
Roots of Manga

Chapter 2 27
Manga Emerges

Chapter 3 42
Shōnen Manga

Chapter 4 55
The Girls' World of Shōjo Manga

Chapter 5 69
Anime

Chapter 6 86
Amerimanga and Americanime

Notes 101

Glossary 104

For More Information 105

Index 107

Picture Credits 111

About the Author 112

Foreword

"Art has no other purpose than to brush aside . . . everything that veils reality from us in order to bring us face to face with reality itself."

—French philosopher Henri-Louis Bergson

Some thirty-one thousand years ago, early humans painted strikingly sophisticated images of horses, bison, rhinoceroses, bears, and other animals on the walls of a cave in southern France. The meaning of these elaborate pictures is unknown, although some experts speculate that they held ceremonial significance. Regardless of their intended purpose, the Chauvet-Pont-d'Arc cave paintings represent some of the first known expressions of the artistic impulse.

From the Paleolithic era to the present day, human beings have continued to create works of visual art. Artists have developed painting, drawing, sculpture, engraving, and many other techniques to produce visual representations of landscapes, the human form, religious and historical events, and countless other subjects. The artistic impulse also finds expression in glass, jewelry, and new forms inspired by new technology. Indeed, judging by humanity's prolific artistic output throughout history, one must conclude that the compulsion to produce art is an inherent aspect of being human, and the results are among humanity's greatest cultural achievements: masterpieces such as the architectural marvels of ancient Greece, Michelangelo's perfectly rendered statue *David*, Vincent van Gogh's visionary painting *Starry Night*, and endless other treasures.

The creative impulse serves many purposes for society. At its most basic level, art is a form of entertainment or the means for a satisfying or pleasant aesthetic experience. But art's true power lies not in its potential to entertain and delight but in its ability to enlighten, to reveal the truth, and by doing so to uplift the human spirit and transform the human race.

One of the primary functions of art has been to serve religion. For most of Western history, for example, artists were paid by the church to produce works with religious themes and subjects. Art was thus a tool to help human beings transcend mundane, secular reality and achieve spiritual enlightenment. One of the best-known, and largest-scale, examples of Christian religious art is the Sistine Chapel in the Vatican in Rome. In 1508 Pope Julius II commissioned Italian Renaissance artist Michelangelo to paint the chapel's vaulted ceiling, an area of 640 square yards (535 sq. m). Michelangelo spent four years on scaffolding, his neck craned, creating a panoramic fresco of some three hundred human figures. His paintings depict Old Testament prophets and heroes, sibyls of Greek mythology, and nine scenes from the book of Genesis, including the Creation of Adam, the Fall of Adam and Eve from the Garden of Eden, and the Flood. The ceiling of the Sistine Chapel is considered one of the greatest works of Western art and has inspired the awe of countless Christian pilgrims and other religious seekers. As eighteenth-century German poet and author Johann Wolfgang von Goethe wrote, "Until you have seen this Sistine Chapel, you can have no adequate conception of what man is capable of."

In addition to inspiring religious fervor, art can serve as a force for social change. Artists are among the visionaries of any culture. As such, they often perceive injustice and wrongdoing and confront others by reflecting what they see in their work. One classic example of art as social commentary was created in May 1937, during the brutal Spanish civil war. On May 1 Spanish artist Pablo Picasso learned of the recent attack on the small Basque village of Guernica by German airplanes allied with fascist forces led by Francisco Franco. The German pilots had used the village for target practice, a three-hour bombing that killed sixteen hundred civilians. Picasso, living in Paris, channeled his outrage over the massacre into his painting *Guernica*, a black, white, and gray mural that depicts dismembered animals and fractured human figures whose faces are contorted in agonized expressions. Initially, critics and the public condemned the painting as an incoherent hodgepodge, but the work soon came to be seen as a powerful antiwar statement and remains an iconic symbol of the violence and terror that dominated world events during the remainder of the twentieth century.

The impulse to create art—whether painting animals with crude pigments on a cave wall, sculpting a human form from marble, or commemorating human tragedy in a mural—thus serves many purposes. It offers an entertaining diversion, nourishes the imagination and the spirit, decorates and beautifies the world, and chronicles the age. But underlying all these functions is the desire to reveal that which is obscure—to illuminate, clarify, and perhaps ennoble. As Picasso himself stated, "The purpose of art is washing the dust of daily life off our souls."

The Eye on Art series is intended to assist readers in understanding the various roles of art in society. Each volume offers an in-depth exploration of a major artistic movement, medium, figure, or profession. All books in the series are beautifully illustrated with full-color photographs and diagrams. Riveting narrative, clear technical explanation, informative sidebars, fully documented quotes, a bibliography, and a thorough index all provide excellent starting points for research and discussion. With these features, the Eye on Art series is a useful introduction to the world of art—a world that can offer both insight and inspiration.

Introduction

Whimsical Pictures

The popularity of Japanese manga, or comics, has exploded around the globe. The manga revolution is being led by a growing pack of world-famous cartoon characters, including gun-wielding pixies, teenage warriors, adorable ogres, frightening soul reapers, and transforming robots. In the United States, Europe, and elsewhere in the West, Japanese manga characters have had a strong influence on popular culture.

Manga is at the center of what journalist Douglas McGray calls Japan's "gross national cool."[1] The unique style of Japanese cool can be seen in street fashion, music, theater, advertising, and graphic arts. Some of Japan's gross national cool comes from the music and fashion business, but much of it originates in the black-and-white pages of manga magazines. Characters like Sailor Moon, Astro Boy, and Doraemon the cat have become superstars in books, video games, live action movies, and animated cartoons, called anime.

Manga is a modern fad, but humorous sketches were first called manga around two hundred years ago. The term, coined by renowned Japanese artist Katsushika Hokusai in 1814, is commonly interpreted to mean "whimsical pictures," but the word has a deeper meaning. As Asian art expert Jocelyn Bouqillard explains, the written Japanese symbol for manga denotes spontaneous drawings made by an artist who is "incoherent, disjointed, confused, or casual." Bouqillard writes that the symbol "suggests rough, rapid sketches—impromptu drawings done on the tide of inspiration, freely and with no sense of order, on a variety of subjects."[2]

In Japan, the inspired, freely created manga comics appeal to almost everyone. Uniformed schoolgirls read romantic comedies, stylish young men in their twenties follow science fiction, and middle-aged businessmen on Tokyo subways read gritty, violent warrior stories. As manga author Daniel Pink writes, "unlike most American comics, [manga] isn't reserved for freaks, geeks, and pip-squeaks."[3] With such widespread

A print from *Thirty Six Views of Mount Fuji* demonstrates artist Katsushika Hokusai's coined term: manga.

appeal, the Japanese manga industry has grown into an immense media business. Publishers annually print more than 1.3 billion manga publications, generating about $4.6 billion.

Unlike American Comics

Manga has been extremely popular in Japan since the late 1940s. In the United States, manga was not available until the mid-1980s. Even then, the Japanese-style comics were slow to catch on because they are completely different from their American counterparts. While American publishers have long sold 32-page color comic books, manga are as thick as telephone books, with 350 pages. Most are printed in black and white. Unlike American and European comics, panel sequencing in manga unfolds on the page from right to left. This often poses a problem for people who learned to read from left to right. To these readers, the comics appear to be printed backward.

There are also artistic differences between American comics and Japanese manga. In the United States, characters are drawn in a realistic manner, whereas Japanese characters have exaggerated features and expressions. When manga characters cry, their tears pour out in torrents. When they laugh, their tiny mouths grow to engulf their faces, while their huge eyes become tiny. An angry character will have steam coming from his or her entire body.

The Japanese Gold Standard

In the twenty-first century, American consumers finally came to embrace the diversity of Japanese manga, and many popular titles have been reprinted in the United States in graphic novels. American manga sales grew from $25 million in 2000 to $175 million in 2007. By 2008, more than half of all graphic novels published in the United States, about fifteen hundred titles, were manga.

In 2010 Japan continued its role as the leading manga producer, but American-made manga, or Amerimanga, was growing in popularity. The style called global manga, created by British, German, Chinese, and Korean manga artists, was also making inroads in the multibillion-dollar graphic novel industry. Despite the growth in other countries, pop culture expert Nicolas Freeman states, "Japanese work is still considered the gold-standard,"[4] because of the nation's extensive manga tradition. As long as worldwide interest remains high, manga will remain atop Japan's production of gross national cool, filling the shelves of bookstores, comic book shops, and libraries for decades to come.

1

Roots of Manga

The Japanese are mad for manga, and Tokyo is the manga capital of the world. The Akiba neighborhood is called the otaku, or "geek" district, because it is filled with superstores that sell manga of all types, from samurai and science fiction to soap operas and fantasy. Loud music pulsates from dozens of manga stores covered in bright strip lighting. Employees stand in front of the multistoried stores, calling out to potential customers through megaphones. Young women dressed as manga characters try to entice readers to browse the shelves. Inside each store, floor after floor is filled with manga, DVDs, games, costumes, and all types of manga-related merchandise, including chocolates, toys, bottled water, clothing, models, playing cards, headphones, and plastic dolls.

Manga publishing is a modern, multibillion-dollar industry based on an ancient art tradition, as American manga expert Frederik L. Schodt explains: "Japanese people have had a long love affair with art (especially monochromatic line drawings) that is fantastic, humorous, erotic, and sometimes violent."[5] The love of single-color, or monochromatic, drawings goes back more than fourteen hundred years to a time when Japan looked to China's highly developed civilization for inspiration.

Tokyo, Japan, is the manga capital of the world, filled with superstores and street sellers that advertise various types of manga.

The Animal Scrolls

In the sixth century A.D., Japan's royal and religious rulers adopted Buddhism from China, and the religion quickly spread among the people. The Japanese also adopted their written language from China. The Chinese do not write words with individual letters but instead use a system of more than fifty thousand graphic symbols, or ideograms, called kanji. Kanji are stylized pictures that express words, phrases, ideas, feelings, colors, actions, sizes, and types of objects. For example, the moon is represented by an ideogram of a crescent moon. Ideograms in the shape of a T or inverted T are used to express the concepts *above* and *below*.

Kanji was useful as a means of recording information, but those who wished to express themselves artistically developed a new form of communication. In seventh-century Japan, artists invented a type of pen-and-ink drawing called caricature, or *fushi* in Japanese. Caricatures are drawings of people that utilize humorous, exaggerated features such as large noses, eyes and ears; giant heads; and tiny bodies. Unlike the complex kanji, caricatures were easily understood by the uneducated public, who could not read. This made simple character drawings useful for entertainment as well as for political or social commentary. Many of the caricatures mocked powerful rulers and wealthy individuals.

Caricatures were a widely accepted form of expression in Japan for many centuries. By the twelfth century, caricatures were so popular they were even used by a respected Buddhist priest, Bishop Toba, to teach religious lessons through art. Toba produced *Chōjū giga*, which translates literally as "humorous pictures of birds and animals." The humorous pictures were drawn on four 80-foot-long rolls (24.3m) of parchment now called the *Animal Scrolls*.

The *Animal Scrolls* contain witty brush-and-ink caricatures of animals engaged in human activities. The birds, foxes, frogs, rabbits, and monkeys are depicted wrestling, bathing in rivers, practicing archery, and praying. In one picture, a frog is dressed as a priest, holding prayer beads and reading from a holy book. Humans also appear in the *Animal Scrolls* in the form of hilarious caricatures that mock the decadent lifestyles of Toba's religious colleagues. Buddhist priests are seen engaged in gambling and playing a game of strip poker.

Modern historians list the *Animal Scrolls* as the prototype of manga. As Schodt explains: "[The *Animal Scrolls* are] Japan's first undisputed masterpiece of cartooning . . . [and] the

BUDDHISM AND ZEN

Buddhism originated in India in the sixth century B.C. and consists of the teachings of the Buddha, Siddhārtha Gautama. It arrived in Japan in the sixth century A.D. but at first was popular only among nobles and aristocrats. Throughout the centuries, Buddhism spread across Japan until a wide majority of Japanese people adopted the religion.

The central theory of Buddhism is that human life is full of suffering due to worldly desires, illness, death, and the loss of loved ones. By ridding oneself of desires and attachments, a person can achieve a state of enlightenment called nirvana. This allows the person to escape suffering.

In 1191, a Buddhist sect called Zen was introduced to Japan from China. In Zen one can achieve self-enlightenment through meditation and self-discipline. Zen philosophy, based on achieving self-enlightenment, is very complex, and the teachings were popular among aristocrats and warriors. However, in the sixteenth century, Zen masters took an interest in the welfare of ordinary Japanese people and began teaching what was called People's Zen. Zen masters used manga-like scrolls filled with caricature and humor to teach their religious concepts to a wide audience.

Buddhism spread across Japan and brought a sect called Zen to the country and its people.

oldest surviving examples of Japanese narrative comic art. . . . [Like manga] of today, changes in time, place, and mood were signified by mist, cherry blossoms, maple leaves, or other commonly understood symbols."[6]

Hungry Ghosts and Hell

Toba's work was among hundreds of picture scrolls created by priests between the late 1100s and the mid-1300s, an era known as the Kamakura period. During this era, which was marked by continuous warfare, most picture scrolls were serious, reflecting the troubled times.

A group of works called the Kamakura scrolls shows hideous monsters and realistic depictions of human beings wracked with genetic defects and disease. These depictions were not created simply to depict unnecessary suffering. They were based on the religious teachings of Buddha.

Buddhists believe that all human suffering is a result of material desires. In order to achieve enlightenment, or nirvana, desire must be eliminated. In Buddhist cosmology, the universe is structured from a number of different worlds, including heaven, hell, and those of humans and animals. A more abstract part of the universe contains "hungry ghosts," earth dwellers who live in deserts and wastelands and who perceive the world differently from humans. Depictions of these various worlds teach lessons about unhappiness caused by material desires and about more abstract concepts such as nirvana.

Scrolls, like this late twelfth-century part of the *Hell Scrolls* series, reflected troubled times. The *Hell Scrolls* used scenes to instruct viewers on how to avoid hell.

The Kamakura scrolls are visual representations of human suffering in the various worlds of Buddhist cosmology. In the *Hungry Ghost Scrolls*, humans who led evil lives are reincarnated, or brought back to life, as starving ghosts. These deformed creatures ravenously eat excrement and dead bodies to survive. This hideous scene was re-created eight centuries later, in the 1970 manga *Ashura* by Jōji Akiyama.

The *Hell Scrolls* are meant to be more instructional. They show viewers pitfalls that should be avoided so they do not wind up in hell. Like today's informational manga, or jōhō manga, the scenes were used to teach. These scrolls were not mass-produced but handmade by individual artists. Because each one is a singular work, the rare scrolls were only available to elite members of Japanese society such as the clergy, nobles, and warrior families.

Zen Humor

The Japanese love of monochromatic line drawings continued to develop within a religious context. A type of Buddhism called Zen, imported from China, was responsible for a new style of art popular in the seventeenth century. Practitioners of Zen believe humans can achieve enlightenment through meditation, self-discipline, and humor. This belief led to humorous religious cartooning called Zenga, or "Zen pictures." These were created by artists for a specific spiritual purpose.

Zen Buddhists believe that enlightenment, called satori, can be achieved suddenly. This can be done by freeing the mind from unnecessary and distracting thoughts, or the world perceived by the senses. This is not necessarily a serious process, as Schodt explains: "The spiritual acrobatics required for such a feat are boosted by an irreverent attitude and a refined sense of the absurdity of [basic survival]."[7]

As a result of this philosophy, Zenga is instilled with humor, freedom, and uninhibited joy. The style is serious, however. Zenga artists attempted to convey profound religious messages about a person's place in the universe. A Zenga master was expected to reveal this philosophy with a few well-placed brushstrokes.

One of the true brushstroke masters of Zenga, a priest named Ekaku Hakuin, began painting around 1740 when he was already in his late fifties. Before his death in 1769, Hakuin produced hundreds of works based on nursery rhymes, humorous poems, and raunchy songs from the red-light district in Edo (now Tokyo). These paintings were created to spread Zen insights to uneducated farmers, laborers, and low-level bureaucrats.

While esoteric by nature, Zenga artists illustrated complex concepts using simple line drawings made with little shading and no colors. They filled the page with words meant to define and embellish their artistic concepts. These defining traits of Zenga—line drawings and words together—are also seen in modern manga.

The Joy of Enlightenment

Gibon Sengai, who became a monk at the age of nine, is another Zen master who did not begin creating Zenga until his late fifties. Sengai roamed Edo, associating with aristocrats, vagabonds, prostitutes, and warriors called samurai. In the early 1800s, Sengai created Zenga using simple lines in black and grey to instruct others about nearly every aspect of life, death, Zen spirituality, and what he called the "joy of enlightenment."[8] Sengai's manga-like characters were often pictured with verses from Chinese and Japanese poems. On some pictures, he added the notation that the work was "playfully sketched."[9]

Sengai mischievously focused on the physical as well as the spiritual side of life. As John Stevens and Alice Rae Yelen explain in *Zenga: Brushstrokes of Enlightenment*: "Sengai did cartoons of people (and Buddhas!) passing wind and answering the calls of nature. . . . Even distinguished abbots [monks] have to answer nature's calls; without their fancy titles and magnificent garments our leaders are the same as any other human being."[10]

Life in Edo

Sengai was a well-loved Zenga artist, but only the elite had access to his handmade work. The most popular drawings of the

SAMURAI WARRIORS

*A*n entire genre of modern manga is based on stories about Japan's famous samurai. This elite class of fighters evolved in the late twelfth century when a warrior chief named Yoritomo created a military government, called a shogunate, in Edo, or present-day Tokyo. By utilizing his military skills, Yoritomo became the nation's first military dictator, or shogun. In doing so, he founded a system of government that was to last almost seven hundred years. The samurai were ruled by a rigid code of honor. They were bound in loyalty to their feudal lord and would defend him to the death. If they failed, they could only redeem their honor by committing ritualistic suicide, or seppuku.

By 1700, over half of Edo's 1.3 million people were samurai. The rest of the city's inhabitants catered to the needs of the warrior class, providing food, clothing, weapons, and a host of other daily necessities.

time were mass-produced for the public by artists in the town of Otsu, between Edo and Kyoto. The artwork, called Otsu-e, had many similarities to modern manga. Otsu-e was produced on cheap paper and featured beautiful women, brawny warriors, and supernatural creatures.

Otsu-e often adorned the walls of the tiny rooms where average people lived in Edo, which had had more than 1 million citizens by 1800. About half of Edo's population consisted of conservative samurai warriors who were part of the military government, called a shogunate. The other half of Edo's population was divided into three distinct classes: court nobles, farmers, and merchants. At the bottom of the social ladder, merchants and townspeople occupied squalid tenements, long row houses constructed of wood. These were built on narrow alleys only 3 feet (1m) wide with open sewers running down

Some of the most popular paintings in past centuries in Japan were called Otsu-e. They were made in the town of Otsu, located between Edo and Kyoto. Otsu-e were sold as souvenirs to passing travelers from stands set along the main road. Created by anonymous artists, the paintings were sold cheaply and in great quantities during the eighteenth and nineteenth centuries. Like modern manga, themes included beautiful women, warrior heroes, animals, and supernatural creatures. Goblins, symbols of evil in Japan, were particularly popular, used to represent human folly. Goblins were shown as drunken, red-faced creatures, symbolizing arrogance, hypocrisy, and carelessness.

Otsu-e were drawn on plain brown paper and colored with blue, red, green, yellow, and white paints. They were mass-produced by artists and their families, including spouses, parents, and children. The artist drew an outline in black, and others filled in the colors with simple brushwork. The resulting pictures were so cheap that almost anyone could afford them. The art was seen attached to doors or glued on walls in a typical home.

the middle of the pathway. Family homes were exceedingly small, about 10 feet by 10 feet (3m by 3m).

The Floating World

To escape their cramped quarters, Edo citizens visited *akusho*, or "bad places," such as theaters, teahouses, bars, and houses of prostitution. Bad places thrived in a huge red-light district called Yoshiwara, established in central Edo by the Tokugawa shogunate in 1617. The district was officially licensed and regulated for men's amusement and diversion. Because this area was a place where men could completely separate themselves from their harsh day-to-day existence, it was commonly known as the "floating world," or ukiyo.

Women known as geisha, literally "artists," were popular entertainers in the floating world, singing, dancing, and playing stringed instruments. Geisha wore white face makeup, beautiful silk kimonos, and flowers in their elaborately styled hair. They were valued for their ability to make interesting conversation with men.

The activities of men and women in ukiyo inspired a type of popular art called floating world pictures, or ukiyo-e. Unlike hand-painted Otsu-e, these multicolor pictures were mass-produced with woodblock printing. Artisans carved the images into wooden blocks, which were coated with colored ink and pressed onto paper, like large stamps. The process allowed printers to create thousands of images from a single block, and the pictures spread quickly throughout society.

There are striking similarities between modern manga and ukiyo-e, according to manga journalist Sheri Le:

> Available as scrolls, greeting cards, book illustrations or single prints, ukiyo-e depicted caricatures of people, landscapes, the uncertainty of life and sensual pleasures . . . in a familiar Japanese style. The aim of ukiyo-e was to capture a feeling rather than depict reality. Artists often focused less on realistic artistic elements and more on introducing humor, eroticism, puzzles, and experiments with line and design to their work. Akin to the manga of today, ukiyo-e was part of Edo period popular culture. . . . It was cheap to produce, widely circulated, and consistent with the spirit of play or entertainment.[11]

Ukiyo-e featured actors, beautiful geisha, and giant sumo wrestlers. (Sumo wrestling was extremely popular in eighteenth-century Edo and remains one of the most beloved spectator sports in Tokyo today.) A very popular type of ukiyo-e, known as shunga, which translates as "spring pictures," showed sexual activities between men and women.

The erotic caricatures of shunga have a modern counterpart in seinen manga. Seinen means "young man," and seinen

Woodblock printing shown with this print of Dainan Gate in Mukden was inspired by the activities of men and women in ukiyo.

manga are created for men eighteen to thirty years old. While not all seinen manga are sexual, many are considered pornographic.

Hokusai Manga

In the early nineteenth century, Katsushika Hokusai emerged as one of the most talented ukiyo-e artists in Edo. Born in 1760, Hokusai was known for his multicolored masterpieces. His subjects include flowers, birds, geisha, samurai, and Mount Fuji, the highest mountain in Japan. Hokusai's ukiyo-e adorned books, calendars, and other items.

Hokusai was fifty-one years old in 1811 when he became the first person to use the word *manga*. The collection he called *Hokusai Manga* consisted of about four thousand amusing images of animals, plants, nature scenes, and supernatural creatures such as gnomes and monsters. The sketches, created in tones of black, gray, and pale flesh, were first published in fifteen volumes in 1814.

Hokusai's sketches were often drawn in the Toba-e style, modeled on the comical pictures created by Bishop Toba. Hokusai's witty caricatures depict people with extremely long, thin legs, limbs, and hands. This drawing style gives the characters a sense of motion and vibrant action.

Hokusai's humorous sketches, along with Toba-e by other artists, were widely distributed in cartoon books called akahon, or "red books" to denote the color of the cover. Printed with woodblocks, akahon have been called the world's first comic books, consisting of twenty or more pages bound by thread. Tobe-e caricatures were used to illustrate traditional children's folktales or fairy tales. The comics also depicted the activities of Edo residents in a humorous fashion. Although the pictures in the akahon were printed in black and white, some readers used paints to hand color and personalize their copies.

East Meets West

Some akahon mocked the government. Such drawings were quickly banned by the Tokugawa shogunate because it was feared the pictures could incite a peasant rebellion. However, the collapse of Japan's feudal military government was not caused by humorous caricatures but by Western forces.

For more than 250 years, the shogunate prevented most foreigners from moving to Japan or even visiting. As the centuries passed, Western influence was kept to a minimum. The shogunate's isolationist policy was forcefully ended in 1853, when the United States sent seven naval destroyers to Edo Bay under the command of Commodore Matthew C. Perry. The commodore threatened to destroy Japanese cities with his

Emperor Meiji brought an era of openness with him as he gained political power.

powerful cannons unless the shogunate opened Japan up to trade with the United States and European nations. Facing total destruction of their coastal cities, the Japanese signed what was known as a friendship treaty. This development brought an influx of foreigners to Japan for the first time in centuries. The power of the shogunate was considerably weakened after its capitulation to the Americans, and the 264-year Tokugawa rule came to an end in 1858.

With the fall of the shogunate, political power was given to Emperor Meiji, who moved the capital from the western city of Kyoto to Edo. He renamed the city Tokyo, or "Eastern Capital." The period known as the Meiji Restoration was marked by an era of openness, where the Japanese welcomed Western culture and technology. Thousands of British, German, American, and French merchants and traders moved to Japan during this period.

Even as Western influences flooded Tokyo, the work of Japanese artists was finding new admirers in Europe. By the 1870s, prints by Hokusai and others had become extremely popular among European painters, including Claude Monet, Vincent van Gogh, Camille Pissarro, Paul Cézanne, and others.

The works of the great Japanese artistic innovators arrived in France in an unusual way. The prints were so cheap and ubiquitous that they were used like newspaper to wrap Japanese handicrafts shipped to European department stores. Monet first spotted Hokusai's work on wrapping paper in an Amsterdam food shop in 1871.

The drawings by Hokusai feature flattened or tilted spaces, vibrant colors, no shadows, and unbalanced or asymmetrical compositions that do not follow traditional Western art standards. This inspired Monet's groundbreaking impressionist painting style, which features open, airy compositions, unusual visual angles, bright colors, and thin brushstrokes.

For the first time in history, Japanese artists strongly influenced Western art. So much so that the term *Japonisme*, or "Japanism" in English, was created to convey the French love for Japanese art. But the influence of Zenga, Toba-e, Otsu-e, and ukiyo-e did more than inspire a group of French painters. The art tradition with roots as old as ancient Japan is alive today in manga sold in Tokyo and other modern cities the world over.

Manga Emerges

In the last decades of the nineteenth century, Japan was rapidly transforming into a modern, industrialized country. As the feudal past was left behind, the new prosperity quickly altered tastes and styles. Western clothes, food, and art were suddenly the rage in Tokyo, and anything imported from the United States or Europe, including comics, was considered superior.

The clash of Eastern tradition and nineteenth-century Western culture gave creators of comic strips in Japan many humorous ideas. According to Frederik Schodt:

> With a new social order and new technologies [from the West] came contrasts and confusion. [Sword carrying] ex-samurai sashayed down streets with top coats and bowler hats . . . and people boarded the first trains after leaving their shoes behind at the station—in keeping with the Japanese custom [of removing shoes] upon entering buildings—only to be shocked when they arrived at their destinations shoeless. It was a cartoonists paradise![12]

The clash of Eastern traditions and nineteenth-century Western culture gave Japanese comic creators many ideas.

Pictures with a Punch

Charles Wirgman, an English illustrator, was one of the Europeans to use the absurdities of daily life in Tokyo as inspiration. In 1862 Wirgman began publishing *Japan Punch*, based on the British humor magazine *Punch*. Published in Yokohama, *Japan Punch* was created in the old akahon, or red-book, style with woodblock printing and bindings stitched with heavy thread.

Wirgman's cartoons in *Japan Punch* made light of everyone, whatever their land of birth. Europeans were portrayed as the Asians viewed them—hairy, overweight, and with big noses. Residents of Japan were depicted as puzzled and amazed when seeing their first bicycle or other Western invention. Japanese leaders were not spared Wirgman's satirical pen. The pages of *Japan Punch* were filled with cartoons mocking government, politics, religion, and law.

As the only English-language humor magazine, *Japan Punch* was very influential among Japan's growing European population. Wirgman's work also provided inspiration to a new generation of Japanese artists. He was the first to use word balloons filled with text, which many Japanese artists adapted to their work. Wirgman's cartoon style came to be known as Ponchi-e, or "Punch-style pictures."

Satirical cartoonist Charles Wirgman was the first to use word balloons filled with text, a detail many Japanese artists began to use in their works.

Sunday Funnies

As the nineteenth century drew to a close, the Sunday funnies were invented in the United States, and the simple comic strips soon extended a broad influence over the world of Japanese cartooning. The fad began in 1895, when renowned newspaper publisher Joseph Pulitzer first ran the cartoon strip *Hogan's Alley* in the *New York World*, a publication with the largest circulation in the United States. The cartoon, which artist R.F. Outcault created for adults, featured a mischievous group of kids living in New York's extensive slums. The wry observations of the characters mocked the class and racial tensions that marked life in the city. The star of *Hogan's Alley* was a bald, bucktoothed character called the Yellow Kid, who wore a yellow, oversized nightshirt printed with cartoon punch lines.

Pulitzer printed *Hogan's Alley* in full color, and the Yellow Kid set off the first cartoon marketing bonanza. The character was featured in plays and vaudeville theatrical skits and was used to sell a range of products that included chewing gum, cigars, dolls, cap bombs, postcards, and even whiskey.

The success of the Yellow Kid attracted the attention of Pulitzer's competitor, William Randolph Hearst, publisher of the *New York Journal*. Hearst started running full-color Sunday comics in his paper that were unique. They were the first comics created with word balloons and four or five panels in a sequence.

Hearst was known for his boisterous self-promotion and advertised the Sunday funnies as: "Eight pages of iridescent polychromous effulgence that makes the rainbow look like a piece of lead pipe!"[13] While it is unclear how many readers understood that "iridescent polychromous effulgence" meant "shimmering, multicolored brightness," by 1906 Sunday funnies, meant to be read by adults and children, were featured in nearly every American newspaper.

American Influence

American-made Sunday funnies were increasingly popular in Japan, especially among creators of Ponchi-e. One such artist, a twenty-four-year-old named Rakuten Kitazawa, began

*A*fter only one year at Joseph Pulitzer's *New York World*, Yellow Kid creator R.F. Outcault was lured to work at a competing newspaper, the *New York Journal*, published by William Randolph Hearst. This ignited a cutthroat competition between Hearst and Pulitzer. Their papers tried to boost circulation by running sensational stories meant to grab the public's attention. Media historian Frank Luther Mott lists some defining characteristics of the type of journalism practiced by Hearst and Pulitzer: "prominent headlines that screamed excitement, often about comparatively unimportant news; a lavish use of pictures, many of them without significance; faked interviews and stories; [and] a Sunday supplement and color comics."

Because the comic *Hogan's Alley* helped ignite the competition between Hearst and Pulitzer, this sort of journalism became known as

"yellow-kid journalism" in January 1897. The term was later abbreviated to "yellow journalism." Today, media that feature sensationalistic stories about celebrities and politicians are referred to as yellow journalism, thanks to the Yellow Kid, who graced the comic pages at the turn of the twentieth century.

Quoted in W. Joseph Campbell. *Yellow Journalism: Puncturing the Myths, Defining the Legacies.* Westport, CT: Praeger, 2001, p. 7.

Thanks to the Yellow Kid comic (pictured) that appeared in newspapers at the turn of the twentieth century, today's sensationalistic media stories are known as yellow journalism.

creating cartoons for an English-language weekly called *Box of Curios*, published in Yokohama. Inspired by the Yellow Kid, Kitazawa introduced the first serialized Sunday comic strip to Japan in 1902. Entitled *Tagosaku and Mokube Sightseeing in Tokyo*, the strip featured two country bumpkins lost in the big city. The full-color strip ran in the Sunday edition of the popular *Jiji Shimpo*, a nationally distributed newspaper.

In 1905 Kitazawa founded a weekly color-cartoon magazine called *Tokyo Puck*. The satirical cartoons in *Puck* attracted widespread attention, and soon the magazine had a circulation of more than one hundred thousand. Kitazawa was fluent in both Eastern and Western comic styles. When he wanted to imitate American funnies, he could use his pen to draw realistic figures with tight lines and accurate perspective. When he wished to convey the Japanese comic style, Kitazawa picked up his brush to create more abstract figures with simple, sweeping lines.

Tokyo Puck made Kitazawa rich and famous. He used his money to travel abroad, visiting New York City in the 1920s. By this time, the Sunday funnies were read by nearly every American who had a penny for a newspaper. Comic strip characters like Little Orphan Annie, Felix the Cat, and Jiggs and Maggie from *Bringing Up Father* were as famous as movie stars and sports heroes. As the popular Japanese cartoonist Ippei Okamoto commented: "American comics have become an entertainment equal to baseball, motion pictures, and the presidential elections."[14]

One of Okamoto's favorite strips was George McManus's *Bringing Up Father*. The comic featured an Irish American named Jiggs, who was a former bricklayer, and his wife, Maggie, a former laundress. Jiggs achieved sudden wealth after winning the Irish Sweepstakes lottery.

In 1923 Okamoto convinced newspaper publishers to begin running *Bringing Up Father* in Japan. He also imported another immensely popular comic, *Felix the Cat*, which featured a mischievous cartoon feline created by Pat Sullivan.

Bringing Up Father was immensely popular and spawned a host of Japanese imitators. Foremost among them was *Easy-*

Japanese cartoonist Ippei Okmoto convinced newspapers in Japan to run the American cartoon *Bringing Up Father*, which led to many Japanese imitations.

Going Daddy, a four-panel strip created in 1924 by Yutaka Aso. *Easy-Going Daddy* was created after the horrific 1923 earthquake that nearly destroyed Tokyo, killing 140,000. The strip featured a lovable middle-aged man who could fix any problem. It was meant to cheer people up after the earthquake, and it was a quick success. Within a year of its appearance, the character Easy-Going Daddy began appearing on merchandise such as dolls and puppets. In later years, the character was a star of books, radio shows, and movies.

Manga for Children

Easy-Going Daddy was primarily created for adults, but the popularity of children's comics had been established a decade earlier. The magazine *Shōnen Club*, or *Boys Club*, first appeared in 1914, and by 1923 it was so successful that the publishers introduced *Shōjo Club*, or *Girls Club*. These Japanese magazines were prototypes for later manga magazines.

Shōnen Club and *Shōjo Club* each had four hundred pages, sold as many as nine hundred thousand copies per month, and featured age-appropriate articles and advertisements. The magazines contained beautifully illustrated comics, which were serialized, or produced in a series, with a new chapter of the comic appearing in each monthly issue.

Manga Propaganda

During the 1920s, Japanese society was as liberal and open as it had ever been. However, as the decade progressed, right-wing militaristic forces gained control over Japan's government. The government clamped down on free speech, censoring and detaining editors, writers, and artists who were thought to be subversive. Artists who criticized the government in their comics were arrested and tortured.

In 1936 the Japanese government joined forces with the Nazi Party controlling Germany, creating the Axis Powers. As the nation moved to build its defenses and prepare for a large-scale war, Japan's military government began using the media, including comic strips, for propaganda.

In the mid-1930s, children's comic magazines began glorifying war in stories featuring Japanese soldiers. Young boys with frightening scowls on their faces were shown carrying guns. The text and pictures instructed children on the values of loyalty, bravery, and strength. Not all prewar comics were serious, however. One of the most popular strips of the 1930s was *Norakuro*, or *Black Stray*, about a stray dog that joins the Japanese Imperial Army, learns to walk upright, and leads other animal soldiers in maneuvers and battle.

On December 7, 1941, the Imperial Japanese Navy bombed the U.S. naval base at Pearl Harbor, Hawaii. The

United States declared war on the Axis Powers and entered into World War II. In Japan, this resulted in wartime rationing. Paper was in short supply, and because of this, most comic books disappeared. Those that remained were used to further the goals of the military government. Stories featured Japanese troops attacking and destroying the American army. *Shōnen Club*, published sporadically throughout the war, became a thirty-two-page propaganda booklet with text and no pictures. The last war issue, dated July 1945, instructed children on techniques for throwing hand grenades.

Ma-chan Launches a Career

World War II ended in unconditional surrender for Japan on August 14, 1945, not long after the United States dropped atomic bombs on two Japanese cities, Hiroshima and Nagasaki. On August 28, U.S. general Douglas MacArthur was made supreme commander of the Allied Powers and was appointed to supervise the occupation of Japan. For the first time in its history, Japan was occupied by a foreign government. Rather than punish its former enemies, however, the United States put a democratic government in place and helped the Japanese rebuild their industrial base.

In the immediate postwar era, the creators of comic strips found a new freedom to express their thoughts. However, the artists were working in an atmosphere that was not conducive to sharp political satire. People were demoralized, hunger was rampant, and death had touched nearly every family. In this atmosphere, people wanted inexpensive entertainment that would cheer them up, and the most popular comics showed humble families with adorable children making the best of a bad situation.

A comic strip that debuted in early 1946, called *Diary of Ma-chan*, perfectly filled the need for lighthearted humor. Drawn by Osamu Tezuka, the four-panel comic followed the humorous experiences of Ma-chan, an energetic, curious eight-year-old boy navigating through daily life in postwar Japan. *Diary of Ma-chan* was an instant hit, and within a few months, wooden Ma-chan dolls were selling at a rapid rate.

NEITHER A COMIC NOR A NOVEL

Osamu Tezuka was the first mangaka to write long, intricate stories, laying the groundwork for today's graphic novels. Helen McCarthy's explanation of the plot from the 1948 Lost World *demonstrates Tezuka's complex story-telling approach:*

[I]n *Lost World*] Planet Mamango was torn away from Earth five million years ago; now it's re-approaching its parent planet and sending down meteorites that generate huge amounts of energy. Boy genius Dr. Kenichi Shikishima is heading for the planet in search of supplies of the stone. Private detective Shunsaku Ban thinks Kenichi holds the key to a murder he's investigating, so he tags along. The party also includes scientist Dr. Makeru Butamo, two attractive but not very intelligent girls created by Makeru from plants, intelligent rabbit Mimio, and stowaway Acetylene Lamp, a journalist. The party finds a prehistoric world where dinosaurs roam among cycads, but their own corruption and greed are the most dangerous things on Mamango. This two-volume story was, as Tezuka remarked on its opening page, "neither a comic nor a novel." A long, complex story with a tragic ending and conflicted characters, this work had been in development since Tezuka was in junior high school.

Helen McCarthy. *The Art of Osamu Tezuka.* New York: Abrams ComicArts, 2009, p. 90.

Tezuka was not yet eighteen at the time, and the popularity of Ma-chan took him by surprise.

Despite his age, Tezuka was already an experienced artist. Born in Toyonaka City, Osaka, in 1928, he created his first comic strip, *Pin-Pin Sei-Cha*, about happy children, when he was nine years old. Growing up, Tezuka loved Japanese manga and American comics. His favorites were *Norakuro* and *Felix the Cat*.

A Movie on a Page

After the success of *Diary of Ma-chan*, Tezuka created a book-length comic, *New Treasure Island*. Tezuka loosely based his two-hundred-page story on *Treasure Island*, written in 1883 by Scottish author Robert Louis Stevenson. His work was unique in several ways. Instead of appearing as a comic strip with flat figures in square boxes, Tezuka used a drawing technique called cinematographic. With this artistic style, the panels flow like scenes in a movie. Helen McCarthy, an authority on Japanese culture and comics, explains:

> The opening sequence of [*New Treasure Island*] is a cinematic tour de force [masterpiece], drawing the reader into the action. . . . Tezuka's huge range of visual . . . references fed into his narrative style and page layout, bringing the "movie" to life on the page. He used pans, zooms, changing viewpoints, and action lines. . . . Tezuka's use of cinematic devices turned the story into a filmstrip and the page into a screen; the reader became the projector.[15]

The public loved Tezuka's cinematic techniques, and *New Treasure Island* was an instant success. Published as an aka-hon, it quickly sold more than four hundred thousand copies. Tezuka followed this achievement with the groundbreaking science fiction trilogy *Lost World*, about scientists traveling to another planet that is populated by dinosaurs.

With *Lost World* and *New Treasure Island* Tezuka revolutionized the comic book industry by creating long, complex stories that went far beyond the four-panel strip. The entirely new concept of combining comic books with novels was explained by critic Tadao Sato: "After Tezuka, it became not at all uncommon to see multi-volume comics with adventure-filled, sustained plots. . . . Tezuka's major achievement was widening the scope of comics, enabling them to achieve the same impact as novels, plays, or any other literary form."[16]

The widened scope required a new word to describe Japanese comics. For reasons unknown, the word *manga*, first coined in the early nineteenth century, came into popular usage. Artists who created manga were called mangaka.

The Mighty Atom and Astro Boy

Tezuka pursued his career as a mangaka with great dedication. He worked long hours, creating thousands of pages of historical works, detective stories, girls' romances, and astonishing science fiction. Whatever the genre of the story, Tezuka's work often contained subject matter concerning peace and environmentalism. He was moved to work these themes into his manga after seeing the horrifying effects of war and the devastation caused by the atom bombs. Through his work, Tezuka came to believe he could convince people to coexist peacefully and take care of the planet. Tezuka's most iconic character, Tetsuwan Atomu ("Mighty Atom" in English), reflects the artist's desire to promote peace.

Tezuka created the Mighty Atom, a boy robot with superpowers, in 1952. In the comic, the Mighty Atom was built by a mad scientist in the far distant future, April 7, 2003. The futuristic Mighty Atom had a nuclear reactor heart, a computer brain, searchlight eyes, a machine gun in his backside, lasers in his hands, and rockets in his feet, which allow him to fly through the air. He was able to understand sixty languages, had super hearing and vision, and could smash through concrete with his one hundred thousand horsepower strength. Despite his awesome powers, the Mighty Atom was also cute and cuddly. And unlike American superheroes fighting for justice, the Mighty Atom fought for equality and peace and mediated between warring factions.

The Mighty Atom was incredibly popular and appeared in his own manga for sixteen years. In 1963 the character starred in Japan's first anime, or animated cartoon series, which was exported to the United States. The Mighty Atom was renamed Astro Boy when he appeared on NBC on Sunday mornings. The character appeared again in 1980 in the anime

Shin Tetsuwan Atomu, or *Astroboy* in other countries. In 2009 the character was revived again in the American computer-animated 3-D film *Astro Boy*.

The God of Comics

Over the years, Astro Boy became a national icon in Japan. On April 7, 2003, the nation celebrated the character's birthday

TEZUKA ON DRAWING

Osamu Tezuka, the "god of manga," forever changed the look of Japanese comics using cinematic techniques. In Manga Manga! *he comments on his artistic methods:*

I felt [after World War II] that existing comics were limiting. . . . Most were drawn as if seated in an audience viewing a stage, where the actors emerge from the wings and interact. This made it impossible to create dramatic or psychological effects, so I began to use cinematic techniques. . . . French and German movies that I had seen as a schoolboy became my model. I experimented with close-ups and different angles, and instead of using only one frame for an action scene or the climax (as was customary), I made a point of depicting a movement or facial expression with many frames, even many pages. The result was super-long comics that ran to 500, 600, even 1,000 pages. . . . I also believed that comics were capable of more than just making people laugh. So in my themes I incorporated tears, grief, anger, and hate, and I created stories where the ending was not always "happy."

Quoted in Frederik L. Schodt. *Manga! Manga! The World of Japanese Comics.* Tokyo: Kodansha, 1997, p. 63.

as imagined by Tezuka when he created the character more than fifty years earlier. Eighty major corporations celebrated the event with toys, books, comics, music, and a baffling array of merchandise, which generated over $5 billion. Beyond the profits his character generated, Tezuka, who died of stomach cancer at the age of sixty in 1989, was lauded as *manga no kami*, literally "the god of comics." The characteristic features seen on his creations, large eyes and button noses, have been imitated by almost every mangaka in the past half century. In a 2007 interview, Schodt, who was Tezuka's friend, explained why the god of comics was able to achieve so much:

Tezuka was a true intellectual, but he began working in a medium of entertainment for children and was able to tailor his ideas to his young audience in a fluid, completely natural way. . . . Tezuka had an almost limitless curiosity about the world, and was amazingly well read. . . . He also loved the theater and had a scientific mind.[17]

Tezuka's brilliance can be seen in *The Complete Manga Works of Tezuka Osamu*, published in Japan. It comprises 80,000 pages in four hundred volumes. While impressive, *The Complete Manga Works of Tezuka Osamu* contains a little over half of the artist's work, which totals 150,000 pages.

The god of comics is honored in the Osamu Tezuka Manga Museum, founded in 1994 in the small town of Takarazuka. But Tezuka's influence remains alive far beyond the museum walls. Born in the ashes of a devastating war, he changed the face of manga. Today, the multibillion-dollar manga industry owes its success to Tezuka, who was influenced by earlier comic creators, including Wirgman, Okamoto, and Aso. Together these artists provided entertainment, social commentary, and joy to countless children and adults throughout a century marked by turmoil and tragedy, progress, and hope.

Shōnen Manga

The first shōnen manga, or comics for boys, appeared in Japan in 1914 and were very popular until the 1940s, when World War II destroyed Japan's publishing industry. After the war, like many other aspects of Japanese society, the manga business sprang back to life with a renewed vigor. In the first eight months of peace after World War II, the number of manga publishers grew from three hundred to over two thousand. The market for shōnen manga was the fastest-growing segment of the postwar manga industry. Shōnen manga, written primarily for males ages eight to eighteen, featured science fiction, superheroes, historical tales, and detective stories.

Tezuka was the leading creator of shōnen manga, producing thousands of pages that featured robots, space travel, samurai warriors, gallant adventurers, and other subjects of particular interest to boys and young men. Tezuka's stories often appeared in the iconic monthly magazine *Manga Shōnen*. The publisher of the magazine, Ken'ichi Katō, was a forward-thinking visionary who understood that there were other gifted young artists like Tezuka among the magazine's readership. To search for new talent, Katō printed a notice in *Manga Shōnen* asking young people to submit short, original comics. Thousands of readers responded with single-panel manga drawn on the backs of postcards.

The editors at *Manga Shōnen* picked out several hundred artists who showed potential. Their submissions were divided into three categories: Winning Comics, Notable Works, and Honorable Mention. Those achieving Notable Works and Honorable Mention had their names printed in *Manga Shōnen*, but the type was so small it could only be seen with a magnifying glass. Artists who produced Winning Comics had their comics published in *Manga Shōnen*. Those who showed the most talent were hired to create serialized stories. While the pay was low, this was considered a dream job. Some contest winners who were hired by Katō, such as Yoshihiro Tatsumi, are now among the most popular and respected mangaka in Japan.

A Jump to Weekly Manga

The popularity of shōnen manga exploded during an era of extraordinary economic growth in Japan. This was coupled with a postwar baby boom. In the years between 1947 and 1952, Japan's annual birthrate nearly doubled, to 2.6 million a year. By 1959, the first Japanese baby boomers were teenagers with money to spend on manga.

Editors at Japan's largest manga publishing company, Kodansha, realized that their eager readers did not want to wait an entire month for the next installment of a favorite comic. In 1959 Kodansha began publishing *Shōnen* magazine on a weekly basis, and there was no shortage of serialized stories to fill the magazine every week. So many popular manga series were available that *Shōnen* magazine quickly grew to over three hundred pages. Other publishers began creating their own weekly offerings, and within a few years Japanese publishers were printing five separate weeklies filled with manga for boys.

Throughout the 1960s, as more baby boomers reached their teenage years, demand for shōnen continued to grow. By 1966, over 1 million copies of *Shōnen* magazine were sold each week. Three years later, that number jumped to 1.5 million. In 1968 the first serious competition to *Shōnen* magazine arrived in the form of *Weekly Shōnen Jump*. This manga magazine was an instant hit and soon began to outsell *Shōnen* magazine.

Shōnen Jump's popularity was driven by controversy. The magazine hired raw rookie artists, who created manga aimed at older males. Artist Go Nagai's *Shameless School* set the tone for the magazine. *Shameless School* was published in the very first issue of *Shōnen Jump*, and it was considered outrageous and offensive. *Shameless School* was a satire on Japan's notoriously high-pressure schools, where students traditionally work very hard and study long hours. Nagai mocked Japan's learning traditions by creating male students and teachers who were obsessed with drinking, gambling, and leering at girls. In an essay in *Japanese Visual Culture*, sociologist Kinko Ito describes her childhood memories of *Shameless School* and the comic's influence on other students:

> [*Shameless School*] was criticized as vulgar . . . and was so controversial that parents publically burned it. Nagai depicted both male students and teachers as preoccupied with catching glimpses of girls. . . . I still remember the days when the boys in my sixth-grade homeroom class started acting out the socially unacceptable actions of Nagai's manga protagonists in a classroom or school-yard. When they were disciplined, the boys claimed that they were just imitating the manga.[18]

Parents' groups such as the PTA tried to have *Shōnen Jump* banned, but the controversy only helped increase the magazine's circulation. Driven by the popularity of *Shameless School* and other controversial manga, *Shōnen Jump*'s weekly circulation hit 2 million. One issue in December 1984 sold a record 4 million copies in one week.

More Work for Artists

The popularity of weekly shōnen manga magazines was a bonanza for the publishing industry but created hardship for mangaka, who now had to create four times as many pages as they did before. Comic promoter Paul Gravett describes how this affected the industry:

Readers quickly came to prefer a weekly "fix" of manga excitement, so monthlies fell out of favor. . . . For manga creators, shifting gears from monthly to weekly publishing schedules quadrupled their workload; the whole working process had to be restructured. To cope, many [artists] set up studios and took on assistants. There were no recognized qualifications in this field, and social status and family connections counted for little. Hence the medium was open to anyone who had talent, luck and drive.[19]

The change to weekly comics also involved a new division of labor. Manga writers were hired to create scenarios and story lines, while mangaka and their assistants created pictures for the stories.

Heads Roll in Samurai Manga

The success of the manga weeklies gave rise to the first generation of male otaku. These comic book geeks, with an obsessive interest in manga, were mainly interested in story themes involving warriors, robots, demons, and athletes. In the warrior category, most manga was inspired by the ancient Japanese samurai tradition. The samurai upheld a strict code, called the Way of the Warrior, or Bushido. The warrior code involved a strong commitment to religion, self-sacrifice, stoicism, and loyalty.

One of the classics in the samurai genre, *Lone Wolf and Cub*, was initially created in 1970 by artist Gōseki Kojima and story writer Kazuo Koike. The story, which took place during the seventeenth-century Tokugawa period, was initially considered controversial because of its vivid violence and sex. *Lone Wolf and Cub* followed the exploits of samurai executioner Ittō Ogami, and nonstop action flowed like blood from page to page. Men fought, heads rolled, and beautiful women were rescued from danger. Even Ogami's baby was involved in the violence, riding in a wooden cart with smoke bombs, spears, and spring-loaded blades to slash his father's enemies.

Drama Pictures

The ninja is another type of Japanese warrior, and these mercenaries can be even more violent than samurai. While samurai are bound by the strict Bushido code, which requires fair play, ninjas do not follow any rules. They use sabotage, espionage, and assassination as well as open combat to achieve their goals. Ninjas are masters of disguise, expert fighters, and insanely violent. This makes them perfect subjects for shōnen manga.

Blood-spattered ninja comics are often drawn in a gritty artistic style known as gekiga, literally "drama pictures." The gekiga genre of serious, dramatic adult manga is meant to depict the grim realities of life in a dark, starkly realistic, violent manner.

The gekiga drawing style is prevalent in modern ninja manga, but it was originally developed for another purpose. In 1957 Yoshihiro Tatsumi invented gekiga to illustrate problems plaguing postwar Japanese society. Tatsumi's early gekiga featured characters such as a father who steals money from his prostitute daughter and an unmarried pregnant woman oppressed by her immoral boyfriend. In a 2009 interview, Tatsumi explained how he came up with gekiga:

> [In the late 1950s, Japan] was getting quite wealthy and things were going really well. . . . Japan was getting rich, but for the people around me, nothing was changing. . . . So I wanted to write some work that expressed the anger and sadness of everyday citizens. . . . I didn't really do anything on the outside, like go out in the world and speak out. Instead, I tried to send some kind of message of protest in my work.[20]

As the inventor of gekiga, Tatsumi is among the most revered mangaka in the world, and his graphic novels are best sellers in Japan, Europe, and the United States. The 2008 graphic novel *Good Bye* features a recent example of Tatsumi's gekiga. The story *Hell* takes place during the final days of World War II. A photographer is sent by Japan's military press bureau to Hiroshima on August 6, 1945, immediately after an atom

Japan is a nation in love with robots. Japanese industry employs over a quarter million industrial robots, more than any other nation in the world. These machines were designed to build cars, appliances, and electronics, but the Japanese are also the leading producers of humanoid robots, meant to perform human functions.

Many Japanese engineers followed robot and mecha manga as children and were inspired to build robots as youngsters. This is the case with those who created Honda's first walking humanoid robot, called ASIMO, introduced in 2001. Honda said the company's inspiration for developing the ASIMO robot was the *Mighty Atom* manga by Osamu Tezuka.

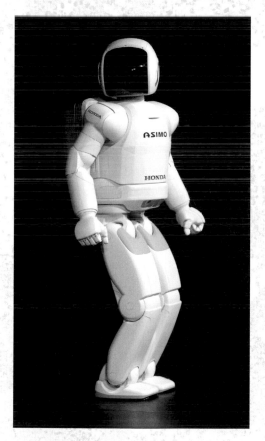

Honda's robot can perform human-like activities like shaking hands, avoiding obstacles, and walking up and down stairs. Improvements are being made so that the robot will have the ability to use its own judgment to perform tasks and to work cooperatively with other ASIMO. In 2008 ASIMO made headlines when it acted as a conductor for a symphony orchestra. For those who grew up with the *Mighty Atom, Iron Man,* and *Mazinger Z,* ASIMO is an example of life imitating art.

Honda's humanoid robot ASIMO was inspired by the Mighty Atom *manga.*

bomb destroys the city. The gritty drawings depict the grisly horror of charred, dead bodies strewn across the wreckage. The story follows a photographer who takes pictures of the horror and remains traumatized twenty-six years after the event.

When Tatsumi invented gekiga, he did so to distinguish his work from child-oriented manga that dominated the marketplace at the time. However, in the decades that followed, the lines between manga and gekiga blurred, as Tatsumi explains:

> [Gekiga] kind of got absorbed by the bigger world of *manga*. . . . [In the 1970s], *manga* was for kids, and *gekiga wasn't* for kids. So to break it down really simply, we don't really use *gekiga* anymore. It's just become a matter-of-fact, natural part of *manga*. But 40 years ago, almost all of the *manga* artists were influenced by *gekiga*.[21]

Robots and Mecha

Whether the stories are created for children or adults, most shōnen manga stories feature a central character, or protagonist, on a personal quest. The manga heroes often have to defeat enemies, but they do so in a setting where they are forced to confront their own weaknesses. They must master their emotions, overcome personal limitations, grow, and mature. This is even true when the protagonists are interactive, drivable, transforming robots or other machines.

The robot fantasy genre is among the most popular shōnen manga in Japan. The stories tend to fall into two categories. Some robots, like the Mighty Atom, are independent, self-directed, and operate free from human interference. When Tezuka created the character, he made up the Ten Principles of Robot Law that the Mighty Atom would adhere to. Among the principles: "Robots are created to serve mankind; Robots shall never injure or kill humans; [and] robots can make anything but money."[22] These Ten Principles gained widespread acceptance among mangaka and have been used for decades in dozens of other stories about self-directed robot characters.

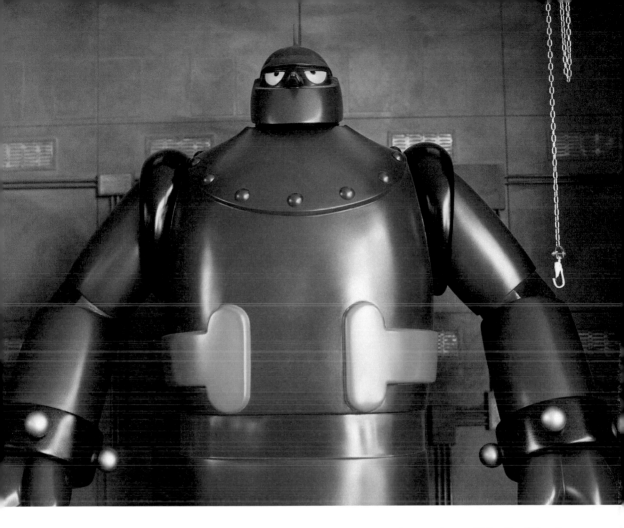

A second type of robot is not self-directed but driven by a human pilot. This type of story is called mecha, short for *mechanical*. The first mecha about a pilot robot was created by Mitsuteru Yokoyama in 1956 to compete with the Mighty Atom. Yokoyama's *Tetsujin 28-gō*, literally *Iron Man #28*, is a giant metal monster that flies through the air with a rocket pack on his back. It is operated by a ten-year-old boy named Shotaro Kaneda using a remote control. The boy's deceased father, Dr. Kaneda, built the robot. Unlike the small, lithe Mighty Atom, Iron Man is a 25-ton creature (22.6 metric tons) that is 92 feet (28m) tall.

Like *Mighty Atom*, *Iron Man #28* was published, republished, and marketed in various ways for years. It was serialized in ninety-seven chapters in *Shōnen* magazine between 1956

Tetsujin 28-gō (literally Iron Man #28) was created to compete with Tezuka's Mighty Atom robot.

CHANGING ROLES FOR WOMEN

For decades, women and girls in shōnen manga were minor characters. However, during the 1990s females began to play increasingly important roles in shōnen manga, as Frederik L. Schodt writes:

Female characters in the comics for men and boys have often been little more than sex objects to be used and abused, or demure, idealized women who serve as [humanizing influences] in plots depicting a harsh masculine world. But times are changing. According to cultural anthropologist Tadahiko Hara, where women in serious dramatic stories were once totally devoted to the man, always ready to sacrifice themselves for his sake, now they are much more passionate and fickle, and are likely to betray the hero. Recent years have also seen an increase in female characters who are quite independent and even eclipse their male counterparts; when sex objects they are often of the Amazongoddess variety [physically strong and powerful]. In the love-comedy stories . . . in boys' magazines, a wholly new type of female has emerged; the American-style "girlfriend" who, in addition to being an object of romantic and sexual interest, is also a best friend and confidante. Usually, she is drawn larger than the male, who is typically small, physically plain, and shy.

Frederik L. Schodt. *Manga! Manga! The World of Japanese Comics.* Tokyo: Kodansha, 1997, p. 75.

and 1966. Since then, it has been collected into a twelve-volume series of books that are rereleased every ten years. A torrent of Iron Man toys and other products have also been produced. Iron Man was adapted into four different anime TV series, the first of which was exported to the United States in 1964 as *Gigantor*. In 2005 *Iron Man #28* was turned into a live-action motion picture, that is, one featuring human actors and not animation.

Mechanical Transformers

Iron Man #28 was the first of many metallic giants, but not all his mecha progeny were controlled by kids. In 1972 Nagai created Mazinger Z, the first monster robot with its own onboard pilot, a young man named Koji Kabuto whose previous experience was racing motorcycles. Mazinger Z, known as Tranzor Z in the United States, was a miracle of engineering, made from an indestructible metal called Japanium. Mazinger Z was built by Professor Juzo Kabuto as a secret weapon against evil mecha, called Mechanical Beasts, created by the wicked Dr. Hell.

When developing the *Mazinger Z* manga, Nagai was strongly influenced by Iron Man #28, which he loved as a child. However, he could not come up with an original idea for a new character until he was stuck in traffic one day. Nagai explains in an interview:

> I was driving along the streets of Tokyo in the middle of a traffic jam where all drivers were sharing a common feeling of anger because they could not move at all. An idea clicked and I started to imagine that my car generated arms and legs to pass all the other cars. I returned to my studio and started to draw and design the first prototypes for Mazinger.[23]

Mazinger Z created a boom in the mecha genre and set the tone for dozens of robot manga that followed. The robot was the first to be piloted by a user within a cockpit. He was described as the only hope for defeating evil and saving the world, and there were several adorable supporting characters such as friends, siblings, and love interests. *Mazinger Z* was the first manga to feature a female robot, Aphrodite A, which is piloted by a woman named Sayaka Yumi. Nagai was the first to introduce a funny robot, Boss Borot, made from old, worn-out parts and garbage.

In the United States, *Mazinger Z* was the inspiration for the 1980s *The Transformers*. This extremely popular animated TV series depicted a war among giant robots that could transform into vehicles, animals, and other objects. *The Transformers* was a marketing phenomenon that inspired a toy line, an

The inspiration for the 1980s' animated series *The Transformers* (pictured as toys) was inspired by the Japanese manga *Mazinger Z*.

album, a theme park ride, a video game, and a Marvel comic book series that was published periodically between 1984 and 2007. *The Transformers* spawned a 1986 animated film, and the transforming robots were featured in three live-action movies between 2007 and 2011.

Ghosts, Goblins, and Vampires

While robot and mecha manga are extremely popular, supernatural stories have also generated great interest among manga readers. These comics feature goblins, ghosts, demons, vampires, monsters, and other paranormal creatures. Supernatural stories are often based on ancient folklore, and like most other shōnen manga characters, the heroes must use self-control to master challenges, no matter how difficult or unworldly the problem.

As with most modern manga, the roots of supernatural comics can be traced back to Tezuka. His series *Dororo*, published between 1967 and 1968, features an orphan girl who teams up with a wandering demon slayer in an artificial body. Together the pair fights thrilling battles against various monsters, a theme that has remained constant in supernatural manga. Some of today's most popular series, such as *Death Note*, *Flame of Recca*, *Bleach*, and *The Demon Ororon*, are about protagonists fighting evil monsters that threaten innocent victims.

Pure of Heart

In the twenty-first century, shōnen manga is the most popular type of comic, accounting for 40 percent of all manga sold

THE *BLEACH* PHENOMENON

Manga series have generated billions of dollars from merchandise in the past half century, but few have matched the success of *Bleach*. Even creator Tite Kubo is surprised by the amazing reception of the manga, which began serialization in Japan's *Weekly Shōnen Jump* in August 2001.

The hero of *Bleach*, Ichigo Kurosaki, is a scrawny high school student with spiky orange hair. His life changes when he accidentally obtains power over life and death as a Soul Reaper. With his new abilities, Ichigo is forced to defend humans from evil spirits while guiding departed souls to the afterlife realm known as Soul Society. As Ichigo learns to control his powers, his friends Sado "Chad" Yasutora and Orihime Inoue accompany him, along with Mr. Yoruichi, a talking cat.

Kubo created over four hundred chapters of *Bleach* between 2001 and June 2010. The chapters have been reprinted in forty-five book volumes, with thirty-one translated into English. These compilation volumes sold over 50 million copies in Japan and have reached the top of manga sales charts in the United States. In addition to manga and book sales, *Bleach* has been adapted into an animated television series and has spawned three animated feature films, numerous video games, eleven CD sound tracks, and an astounding five theatrical rock musicals.

in Japan. *Shōnen Jump* is the best-selling publication, with a weekly edition typically selling 3 million copies or more. Toys, candy, clothes, and other products bearing images of shōnen manga characters generate billions of dollars. These products are sold in almost every department store, supermarket, and train station in Japan.

To some Westerners traveling in Japan, the popularity of manga seems inexplicable. Tourists often marvel at the sight of businessmen on commuter trains absorbed with reading the latest shōnen manga. They wonder how grown men, husbands and fathers, can be interested in comics mainly created for boys and teenagers. Gravett offers his explanation for this phenomenon:

> What seems to sell *Shōnen Jump* and other titles to boys of six to 60 is their values of friendship, perseverance—and winning. In weathering the struggle of rebuilding their country since the war, and now of reviving their economy since the recession, the Japanese have continued to find inspiration and solace in shonen manga heroes. It's somehow fitting that that word *shonen* not only means "boy," made up of the characters for "few" and "years," but also "pure of heart."[24]

The Girls' World of Shōjo Manga

W hen Machiko Satonaka was growing up in the early 1960s, she was a talented artist. Satonaka was also a big fan of shōjo manga, or girls' comics, created for female audiences between the ages of eight and eighteen. Satonaka dreamed of the day when she could create manga for shōjo magazines such as *Ribbon* and *Shōjo Friend*. At the time, however, shōjo manga was created by men. Satonaka questioned this situation, wondering why women were not involved in creating shōjo manga. She says,

> I thought I could do a better job myself, and that women were more capable of understanding what girls want than men. Drawing comics was also a way of getting freedom and independence without having to go to school for years. It was something I could do myself, and it was a type of work that allowed women to be equal to men.[25]

In 1964 Satonaka entered an amateur mangaka contest held by *Ribbon*, a magazine produced by Japan's biggest publisher, Kodansha. Much to her surprise, Satonaka's vampire manga, *Portrait of Pia*, won the prestigious New Cartoonist Award. This launched her career as a professional mangaka when she

Shōjo manga were comics created for females between ages eight and eighteen.

was sixteen years old and still in high school. A year later, Satonaka dropped out of school and moved to Tokyo to create shōjo manga full-time. In the decades that followed, Satonaka created a number of award-winning manga series, including *Shining Tomorrow*, *There Goes the Princess*, and *The Hunter's Constellation*.

The Magnificent 24s

Satonaka began her career as the manga industry was growing at a dramatic pace. *Shōnen* magazine was selling millions of copies each week, and Kodansha decided comics for girls could be equally profitable. The company began publishing the weekly *Shōjo Friend* in 1962. Satonaka's first professional comic appeared on the pages of *Shōjo Friend* two years later.

The success of *Shōjo Friend* prompted other publishers to produce shōjo manga weeklies. Within a few years, magazines such as *Margaret* and *Shōjo Comic* were competing with *Shōjo*

Friend. As had happened in the shōnen manga sector, the growing popularity of shōjo weeklies increased the demand for artists. Major publishers decided that women mangaka were more likely to attract a loyal female audience. Most shōjo weeklies stopped publishing series created by men and began hiring female mangaka.

The switch to women artists helped increase shōjo magazine sales, and by the end of the 1960s, dozens of female mangaka had become famous for creating girls' comics. Newspaper articles about the rise of female mangaka referred to the new generation of women artists as the Fabulous Forty-Niners. The term was used because most of the artists were born in or around 1949. In 1973 the artists were given another nickname because they were all around twenty-four years old at the time. The female man gaka came to be called the *Showa 24* (Year 24 Group), or the Magnificent 24s. In the twenty-first century, this nickname is a term of deep respect because the influence of the Magnificent 24s can be seen in nearly every modern shōjo manga.

Taboo Subjects

The Magnificent 24s includes a group of venerated Japanese artists, including Moto Hagio, Riyoko Ikeda, Yumiko Oshima, Keiko Takemiya, and Ryoko Yamagishi. Like their male counterparts, the Magnificent 24s created stories in numerous genres. For example, in the 1970s, Moto created *The Heart of Thomas*, a melodramatic romance, and *The Poe Family*, a supernatural historical drama with vampires. Moto's most popular work from the era, *They Were Eleven*, is a science-fiction tale about young space cadets whose survival skills are tested on a decommissioned space station.

As pioneers in their field, the Magnificent 24s felt less bound by traditional rules. Some addressed controversial themes that male shōjo artists had long avoided. Ikeda's 1975 *To My Respected Elder Brother . . .* is about a sixteen-year-old girl, Nanako Misonoo, who describes her high school experiences in a series of letters to her brother. The thirty-nine-chapter series shocked readers when it explored themes relating to incest, suicide, lesbianism, drug addiction, and divorce.

Ikeda's story was created for baby boomer readers who were reaching their late teens and early twenties at the time. It was among a group of shōjo manga that dealt with activities considered taboo in Japanese society. Homosexuality, in particular, was previously unmentionable in the world of manga. But the mangaka of the Magnificent 24s were fearless when it came to exploring the sexuality of characters.

This character illustration of Queen Marie-Antoinette was created by Riyoko Ikeda, one of the Magnificent 24s.

Keiko Takemiya is renowned as a member of the Magnificent 24s and as creator of the pioneering science fiction/fantasy *Toward the Terra*. In 2000 Takemiya joined the faculty of Kyoto Seika University's Faculty of Arts, where she helped found the School of Manga. This is the only four-year institution in Japan that offers courses on creating manga.

The School of Manga trains students in drawing techniques and the history of manga. Courses offer instructions in single-panel cartoon manga and story manga told through a series of frames. Commenting on her transformation from best-selling mangaka to university professor, Takemiya stated, "When I first became a *manga* artist I thought the techniques were something that couldn't be taught, but I've come to want to pass them on in some form."

Quoted in Deb Aoki. "Interview: Keiko Takemiya." About.com. http://manga.about.com/od/manga artistswriters/a/KeikoTakemiya_2.htm.

By the 1980s, so many manga series had been created with gay characters that the topic was no longer considered shocking. Stories focusing on homosexual romances created by female artists for female readers were so common they were referred to simply as "boys' love" and "girls' love" manga.

Unchained Panels

Whatever the genre, most shōjo manga of the 1980s featured similar themes, and the stories followed the same basic pattern. Female characters were usually passive heroines dealing with love and loss. As Frederik Schodt explains: "Most [manga series] were melodrama starring young girls, often waifs and tomboys. Plots progressed [inevitably] towards a joyful 'union' with lost parents, a boyfriend, or man in marriage, or a tragic 'separation,' usually through death."[26] Shōjo romance stories could be extremely long, with some, such as Satonaka's *Tomorrow Will Shine*, stretching to over one thousand pages.

Beyond the story lines, the Magnificent 24s invented a unique artistic style more appealing to female sensibilities. While male artists drew square, linear panels, women went beyond the rectangular boundaries, as Gravett explains:

> Men's logic and linearity were overruled. The generation of female mangaka unchained their panels from the uniformly regimented rectangles and rows beloved of the male creators. They gave their panels whatever shape and configuration best suited the emotions they wanted to evoke. They softened the ruled borders outlining their panels, sometimes breaking them up, dissolving them or removing them altogether. They overlapped or merged sequences of panels into collages. A borderless panel could now permeate the page, often beneath flotillas of other panels sailing across it, or it could expand or "bleed" off the edges of the printed page itself and imply an even bigger picture beyond the paper. Thus time and reality were no longer always locked up inside boxes and narratives could shift in and out of memories and dreams. Characters too were no longer always contained within panels, but could stand in front of them, sometimes shown in full length.[27]

Enormous Eyes

Female mangaka incorporated other stylistic elements that made their work noteworthy. For example, female characters were drawn with huge, round, doll-like eyes and extremely long eyelashes. In the early 1980s, male reviewers criticized this style, writing that the giant saucer eyes were ludicrous and a sign of poor drawing skills. Female mangaka responded, saying male reviewers misunderstood the function of eyes in shōjo manga. As Japanese art and culture expert Mizuki Takahashi explains:

What these critics overlooked was that the main purpose of shōjo manga was to show the complex inner psychology of the characters, not to create a realistic or action-filled tale. The aesthetic features, such as enormous eyes with long eyelashes, full-body portraits, and complicated panel designs are crucial for fans to engage emotionally with the story. . . . In regard to what these eyes signify, some have argued that starry eyes symbolize the love and dreams of the characters. . . . [They] also serve as mirrors that reflect the character's emotions. In other words, the eyes literally are the windows of the soul; by looking at the eyes, the readers can intuit the character's feelings, which remain unexpressed in dialog.[28]

The round, large, doll-like eyes of female characters were one of many stylistic elements incorporated in female mangaka.

WOMEN DRAWING FOR MEN

While most female mangaka create shōjo manga, some women artists have achieved spectacular success drawing shōnen comics for males. Rumiko Takahashi is one such artist, and her manga made her one of the richest people in Japan.

Takahashi began drawing comics while attending college. She self-published her first works in 1975 but did not work professionally until 1978, when she created *Urusei Yatsura*, a series that combines humor, science fiction, and romance. After Takahashi created this well-received shōjo manga series, she began drawing seinen manga, comics for males ages eighteen to thirty, which were published in *Shōnen Sunday* magazine. Takahashi went on to achieve great success with the fantasy manga *Mermaid Saga* and the martial arts manga *Ranma*. While these series appeal to male readers, the women in Takahashi's manga are strong-willed and powerful, not the subservient sex objects often seen in seinen manga. Over the course of her career, Takahashi has sold over 100 million copies of her work in books, and her characters have appeared in anime and on countless types of merchandise.

The enormous eyes of a shōjo character can take up half of the character's extremely large head, which itself might fill the entire page. This drawing style is used to show subtle expressions that demonstrate a character's inner thoughts, intimate feelings, and psychological makeup.

Fashion and Flowers

To keep the focus on the emotions shown in the face, female bodies are often drawn with much less detail. However, nearly every shōjo manga chapter features at least one full-body portrait of a central character in the middle of a page. Male critics sometimes disapprove of these portraits, considering them an interruption in the story, but shōjo fans do not think of them as an intrusion. As Takahashi writes, "Part of their allure for women has always been that they were all about fashion—full-body images appear on the page like mannequins modeling the latest ensembles in store windows."[29]

Beyond the physical features of characters, female mangaka give depth to a story by adding illustrations of flowers. Japan has an ancient tradition of using flowers as symbols in religious and social settings. For example, the lotus flower is used in Buddhism to represent purity of body, speech, and mind and may be used to represent ideal feminine attributes of beauty, perfection, and grace. Peonies are associated with happiness and prosperity, cherry blossoms with loyalty, roses with sensuality, and irises with strength, vitality, boldness, and power.

Flowers are among the many symbols used by female mangaka to depict love in a refined manner. Schodt explains:

> [Girls'] comics have an unstated rule . . . that all subjects, no matter how decadent, must be depicted with delicacy. Today's women artists are therefore masters of . . . suggestion. Unfolding orchids and crashing oceans are superimposed on scenes of lovers embracing. Close-ups of . . . tousled hair and sweating faces allow the reader to imagine the rest.[30]

Josei Manga

One genre of shōjo manga goes beyond subtle depictions of love and is comparable to graphic seinen manga, or "young man comics." Josei manga, literally "ladies' manga," first appeared in the early 1990s. This style was originally created for housewives and what the Japanese call "office ladies," or young clerical workers.

Josei manga is often compared to American soap operas. The stories feature numerous love affairs, quarrels, betrayals, spurned children, crimes of passion, and other melodrama. The genre was originally created for women eighteen to twenty-eight years old, but the mature storytelling also appeals to high school girls who buy josei manga magazines such as *You* and *Kiss*.

One of the most successful serialized josei manga stories, *Honey and Clover*, was created by artist Chica Umino. The series, which ran from 2000 to 2006, follows students who live in the same apartment building and attend a Tokyo art college. *Honey and Clover* uses comedy and drama to portray romances, love triangles, broken hearts, job searching, and other difficulties experienced by the art students. The series was so successful that it was adapted as an anime TV series in Japan, something that is rare for the josei genre. *Honey and Clover* was also the basis for a live-action movie.

Sailor Moon

In Japan, young girls are given shōjo manga as soon as they learn to read, and many of today's most renowned female mangaka grew up reading *Banana Bread Pudding*, *They Were Eleven*, and other manga of the Magnificent 24s. One of these artists, Naoko Takeuchi, born in 1967, began drawing comics in high school and joined her school's Manga Club around that time. Although Takeuchi went on to attend college, she decided to forgo a career as a pharmacist to draw manga for Kodansha at the age of nineteen.

In 1991 Takeuchi created *Codename: Sailor V* about a thirteen-year-old middle school student, Minako Aino, who dreams about finding true love. However, Aino's life changes dramatically when she meets a talking cat that tells her she has powers to transform into a superwoman named Sailor Venus, or Sailor V. In the guise of Sailor V, Aino fights evildoers who are part of the Dark Agency.

The popularity of *Codename: Sailor V* inspired Takeuchi to create a series about a team of magical girl heroines that have both normal and magical identities. The girls, named after planets and moons, work with Sailor V to fight evil in outer space. The result was *Pretty Soldier Sailor Moon*, widely known as *Sailor Moon*. The series is named after the team's leader, Sailor Moon, whose blonde hair tied in a double-bun style place her among the most recognizable manga characters.

Since its creation, *Sailor Moon* has become one of the most popular comic series ever created. The fifty-two chapters of the

The manga publishing world is highly competitive, and magazines may achieve incredible popularity one year and disappear from the newsstands the next. However, *Nakayoshi*, or *Best Friend*, magazine has managed to avoid that trend, selling around four hundred thousand copies every month. First published in December 1954, the magazine for girls between the ages of nine and fourteen is the world's longest-running manga magazine. For around five dollars, readers can buy the 450-page "phone book manga" filled with twelve to fifteen serialized *shōjo* manga series. *Nakayoshi* also comes with *furoku*, or small gifts, including stickers, posters, small shopping bags, cardboard carrying boxes, and games.

Nakayoshi is most famous for being the first to serialize *Sailor Moon* in the 1990s. But other popular manga series, such as *Sugar Rune*, *Mermaid, Melody & Tokyo*, and *Mew Mew*, have appeared on the magazine's pages.

The world's longest-running manga magazine, Nakayoishi (Best Friend), *was the first to popularize and serialize* Sailor Moon.

series ran in the shōjo manga magazine *Good Friend* from 1992 until 1995. It was later serialized in eighteen volumes, which sold over 1 million copies each in Japan. The books were exported to over twenty-three countries, including China, Mexico, Australia, and those in Europe and North America. These volumes were rereleased in 2003 when a live-action series based on the manga, called *Pretty Guardian Sailor Moon*, ran on Japanese TV.

The *Sailor Moon* anime began airing only a month after the first issue of the manga was published and was seen in two hundred episodes before it ended in 1997. Because of its previous popularity, the anime series was back on the air in 2009. There were also three theatrically released movies: *Sailor Moon R: The Movie*, *Sailor Moon S: The Movie*, and *Sailor Moon SuperS: The Movie*. In addition, *Sailor Moon* ignited a marketing bonanza, with the series characters appearing on over five thousand different types of merchandise.

"Drop-Dead Hunky Guys"

The popularity of *Sailor Moon* has been credited with the amazing twenty-first-century boom in mahou shōjo, or "magical girl manga," such as *Searching for the Full Moon* and *Twin Princesses of the Wonder Planet*, which first appeared in 2005. Magical girl manga features young girls with superhuman abilities who must fight evil forces to protect the earth. Like many superheroes, they possess secret identities and obtain their powers from a magical object such as a pendant, wand, or ribbon. A magical girl will often have a talking pet as a sidekick and will work with others of her kind, in superpower teams that work against evildoers.

The magical girls subgenre is part of the supernatural style that includes vampires. *The Vampire Knight* by Matsuri Hino merges several classic manga themes, vampires, gothic horror, and high school romance. The story revolves around Cross Academy, where the Night Class is full of attractive vampires. The Day Class does not know the others are really bloodsuckers. One of the students, a girl named Yuki, knows about the monsters because she was saved from them by one of them as a small child. She has become one of the school's guardians, keeping the two groups apart no matter how attractive the Night Class is to those in the Day Class.

Hino began the series in 2005, and it continued to run for more than five years. She told the story using dark panels crowded with dramatic gothic art. Cartoonist and manga reviewer Deb Aoki lists *The Vampire Knight* among her "Top 10 Shojo Manga Must-Reads," noting the series is full of "Gorgeous artwork, drop-dead hunky guys . . . [which] make this a favorite for readers who love romance with a dark side."[31]

"Goofy Romantic Comedy"

Fruits Basket is a more lighthearted series that combines the supernatural with romance. The popular series follows high school student Tohru Honda after her mother dies in a car accident. Honda moves in with her classmate Yuki Sohma only to discover his wealthy family lives with a curse. The thirteen members of the family are possessed by spirits of the Chinese zodiac, represented by animals such as the rat, ox, tiger, snake,

Manga artist Natsuki Takaya created the lighthearted series *Fruits Basket*.

monkey, dog, and dragon. The characters in the manga turn into their zodiac animal when hugged by members of the opposite sex. Honda tries to break the curse and ends up changing the family forever. Commenting on the strip, Aoki writes, "*Fruits Basket* starts off as a goofy romantic comedy, then develops into an emotional roller coaster that mixes humor, fantasy, profoundly emotional romance and family drama for an addictive mix that has made it the best-selling *shojo manga*."[32]

Slow Pace, High Sales

In Japan nearly all preteen girls regularly read manga, along with three-quarters of teenagers and more than half of all women under the age of forty. They start out with shōjo manga for young girls, such as *Nakayoshi* or the top-selling magazine *Ciao*, and graduate to *Cookie* as teenagers. Those who remain interested in manga as they grow older have numerous josei manga offerings to chose from, including *Chorus*, *Elegance Eve*, and *Office You*.

By conforming to the tastes of female readers, shōjo manga books and magazines generate billions of dollars every year. The romantic comedies such as *Boys Over Flowers* by Yoko Kamio and *Glass Mask* by Suzue Miuchi each sold over 50 million copies during the decades they were published, first as serialized manga, then as collected volumes reissued nearly every year.

As sales figures show, female mangaka have exerted a positive and lasting impact on shōjo manga. Art created by women for women, which was considered revolutionary in the 1960s, is a matter of fact in the twenty-first century. The work of the Magnificent 24s made a lasting impact on generations of readers and continues to resonate today.

Anime

On March 18, 2008, Japanese foreign minister Masahiko Komura held a news conference accompanied by a human-sized Doraemon doll. Doraemon is a cartoon robot cat with a magical pouch and is a huge celebrity in Japan. The blue-and-white cat stars in an animated cartoon, or anime, about a boy in the twenty-second century who is sent back to the present day to aid his unlucky grandfather.

During the 2008 news conference, Komura named Doraemon as Japan's "anime ambassador." The cat was given an official government certificate signed by Komura that stated, "Doraemon, I hope you will travel around the world as an anime ambassador to deepen people's understanding of Japan so they will become friends with Japan."[33] Doraemon responded through the voice of actress Wasabi Mizuta, stating, "Through my cartoons, I hope to convey to people abroad what ordinary Japanese people think, our lifestyles and what kind of future we want to build."[34] After the official ceremony, Doraemon's favorite dessert, *dorayaki*, or red bean pancakes, was served.

Doraemon, which roughly translates as "stray cat," was created by Hiroshi Fujimoto and Moto Abiko, who worked together under the pen name Fujiko Fujio. The series was published as a

Moto Abiko (pictured) worked with Hiroshi Fujimoto under the pen name Fujiko Fujio.

manga for more than two decades, from 1969 until 1996. Like many popular manga series, *Doraemon* spawned several theatrical musicals, video games, animated feature films, and three separate anime series that total more than sixteen hundred episodes. As a result of its popularity, *Doraemon* is one of the biggest names in Japanese pop culture, despite the fact that the anime was created for a grade-school audience.

The First Anime

Animated cartoons are a multibillion-dollar business, and about 60 percent of all anime features created in Japan are based on successful manga. Journalist Simon Richmond describes anime as featuring "doe-eyed, spiky-haired youths, giant laser-blasting robots, nifty-footed ninjas and cuddly little monsters."[35]

Richmond notes that computer-generated images in Japanese anime have become as much a part of world culture as Madonna and iPods. But long before the invention of MP3 players, or even rock and roll, Japanese artists were creating animated films that represented their own unique view of the world.

The first animated films were created around 1900 in the United States, and the earliest examples of Japanese anime were made in 1917. The anime *The Monkey and the Crab* and *Momotarō* were created by *Tokyo Puck* artist Seitaro Kitayama. Like countless manga stories, the animated films were based on ancient Japanese folktales.

The Disney Effect

While a few anime were made in the prewar era, the business did not begin to grow until 1948, when Toei Animation was founded. At that time, the most popular animated films in Japan were now-classic works produced by Walt Disney Studios in Burbank, California. Disney's animated films had realistic human animation, unique characters, special effects, and bright, vivid colors. These features made cartoons like *Cinderella*, *Alice in Wonderland*, and *Peter Pan* the most distinctive animated films of the 1950s.

Although Disney was the worldwide king of cartoons, Toei decided to challenge the studio with its own feature-length, full-color anime films. In 1958 the studio produced *The Tale of the White Serpent*, based on an eleventh-century Chinese folktale, using the style Disney made famous. The film, about a young boy whose pet snake turns into a beautiful princess, was filled with musical numbers and talking animals. It was released in 1961 as *Panda and the Magic Serpent* in the United States. The Toei studio continued to create films in the

I t is sometimes difficult for Westerners to understand the respect some Japanese people hold for animated cartoon characters, but the reverence can be traced to ancient traditions. Most Japanese people believe in spirits called *kami,* which inhabit natural objects such as mountains, waterfalls, trees, and animals. In the eighteenth century, respected Japanese scholar Motoori Norinaga described the *kami* as "anything whatsoever which was outside the ordinary, which possessed superior power or which was awe-inspiring. . . . Evil and mysterious things, if they are extraordinary and dreadful, are called *kami.*" These elements of religion and mythology are central to anime and manga, and many series, such as *My Neighbor Totoro* and *Princess Mononoke,* feature characters indentified as *kami.* Because inanimate objects, even cartoon cats, are said to have their own life force, characters such as Doraemon are perceived as *kami* because of their extraordinary, awe-inspiring powers.

Quoted in R.H.P. Mason and J.G. Caiger. *A History of Japan.* Rutland, VT: Charles E. Tuttle, 1997, p. 33.

Kami—spirits that inhabit natural objects—are central to anime and manga series like Princess Mononoke.

Disney style but is best know today for the anime it produced in later decades, including the *Dragon Ball* (1986), *Sailor Moon* (1992), and *Digimon* (1999).

Tezuka Gets the Bug

During the late 1950s. Toei employed Osamu Tezuka as a director and screenwriter for two feature-length anime, *The Adventures of Sinbad* and *Doggie March*. But Tezuka believed there was more money to be made in television anime. This led him to found his own animation studio in June 1961. Tezuka named his studio Mushi Productions, literally "Bug Productions," after his favorite creature, the insect.

Mushi's first film, the thirty-eight-minute *Stories of a Street Corner*, was not made in the cheerful Disney style. *Stories of a Street Corner* is about a pending war that threatens to destroy the world. The story is told not by human characters but through animated posters on a wall. The anime was inspired by traditional Japanese beliefs that state that inanimate objects such as plants, or even posters on a wall, have their own life force. As McCarthy writes, this ancient belief was melded with new thinking that evolved in the 1960s: "[The film's] central message anticipated the mood of a new decade: celebrate life. Or put another way, make love, not war."[36]

Although Tezuka would go on to make seven more experimental films in the 1960s, most of his time was spent creating his famous anime *The Mighty Atom*. Tezuka began making plans for an anime TV show based on the character in 1962 at a time when the American cartoon *The Flintstones* was being shown in Japan. Unlike the intricately drawn Disney cartoons, *The Flintstones* was created quickly using fewer drawings and cheaper production techniques. Tezuka used the cartoon as a production model for *The Mighty Atom*.

Making Astro Boy Fly

On January 1, 1963, *The Mighty Atom* debuted on Fuji TV in Japan. The show was an instant hit. The success of *The Mighty Atom* came with a price, however. Tezuka's deal with Fuji TV required him to produce the cartoon on a tight schedule with

The artistic changes made to *The Mighty Atom* as it moved from the page to the screen earned its creator Osamu Tezuka the nickname "God of Manga."

an extremely low budget. Richmond describes the problems that resulted: "Tezuka's team was not only being poorly paid but also being pushed to their physical limits to create the series on time. Artists later recalled how their fingers blistered and bled from constant work and how they slept under their desks rather than returning home."[37]

In order to produce *The Mighty Atom* as cheaply as possible, Tezuka invented production techniques that soon became industry standards. During this era, animation was produced with individual drawings made on transparent sheets of film called cels. (*Cels* is short for *celluloid*, the colorless plastic film on which drawings were made.) Artists created the illusion of movement by drawing an image on a cel. Another cel was laid on top of the original, and the arms, legs, mouth, or eyes of the character would be moved very slightly. As more cels were layered onto one another, the character appeared to speak, blink its eyes, and make other movements. Companies like Disney created twelve different cels for every one second of movie film.

To cut costs, Mushi created anime with only eight drawings per second of film. This resulted in jerky character movements. To cut production costs further, the characters in *The Mighty Atom* were drawn with only three mouth positions, open, shut, and half-open. Sometimes characters would speak but their backs were to the camera, so no animation was necessary. This was unlike Disney cartoons, where the characters had at least a dozen different mouth movements when they were speaking.

Modern viewers can watch 1960s episodes of *The Mighty Atom* and *Astro Boy* at various websites on the Internet. While the jerky motion and lack of sophistication is a result of cost cutting, it gives the anime a unique charm and style that some say is missing from high-tech computer animation.

Beyond production techniques, Tezuka updated and changed the artistic style of his famous robot. According to Frederik Schodt, the Mighty Atom "became more modern and 'cute'"[38] to appeal to boys in elementary school. In addition to portraying the Mighty Atom as a friendlier character, anime allowed the robot to speak for the first time. Fans could also listen to explosions, screams, and other special sound effects that could only be imagined when read on the page.

Whatever the artistic changes when *The Mighty Atom* moved from the page to the screen, it was so popular that Tezuka earned a new nickname. Throughout the 1950s, he

CREATING ANIMATION

Until computers took over many aspects of anime production in the early 1990s, animated films were created when individual drawings, paintings, or illustrations were made on a transparent sheet of film called a cel (short for *celluloid*). In this process, characters on each cel differ slightly from the one preceding it. The illusion of movement is achieved when the cels are photographed on movie film, which allows them to be projected in rapid succession.

Photographing cels frame by frame is called stop-frame cinematography. In high-quality cartoons, like those produced by Walt Disney Studios, cartoons were shot at twenty-four frames per second. In this process, twelve slightly different cels are made for each twenty-four frames, or one second, of film. This was an extremely time-consuming and costly process but delivered a realism that was previously unmatched in animated films.

In the 1960s, cheaper animation, with eight cels per second, was used for cartoon series like *Astro Boy* and *The Flintstones*. Although the character movements were jerky, this technique allowed producers to create cartoons faster, which meant they could be broadcast on a weekly basis.

was known as the "god of Manga" for his groundbreaking drawing techniques. With the popularity of his flying cartoon robot, Tezuka was widely referred to in the press as the "god of anime." The success of the show spawned dozens of imitators; by 1964 three new animation studios opened in Tokyo, and within a year, five new anime series appeared on Japanese TV.

As the popularity of anime TV series continued to grow, the shows, like manga, divided along gender lines. Shōnen anime for boys featured monster robots and violent warriors. In the field of shōjo anime, the first of the magical girls was introduced with *Princess Knight*. This series featured a brave female heroine who dressed like a boy when she fought evil.

Artistically, the visual appearance of anime transformed dramatically after the introduction of color television in the mid-1960s. Familiar black-and-white characters from the pages of manga appeared in full color for the first time. Besides adding a new visual dimension to the anime, color could now be used in a symbolic manner to inform viewers about a character's personality. This has been particularly true with hair color. For example, as anime expert Antonia Levi states, blonds in anime "are frequently either deliberate instigators of trouble or at least unwitting sources of chaos. . . . Watch out for blonds! They're usually a sign of trouble if not actual evil."[39]

Changes in Technology

The addition of color gave anime a new artistic quality, but production and distribution had changed little over the years. Artists toiled over thousands of cels for long hours, while the finished anime were shown on TV or at movie theaters. Several technological developments in the 1980s changed this decades-old business model. The first was the mass production of inexpensive videocassette recorders and cheap VHS tape by Japanese companies like Sony. In the early 1980s, movies became available on VHS tape for the first time. This inspired anime artist Mamoru Oshii to take advantage of this new technology. Oshii decided to sell his science-fiction anime *Dallos* only on VHS tape in 1983. This form of videotape

The anime *Golgo 13: The Professional* marked the beginning of the computer-generated images (CGI) era.

anime became known as original video animation (OVA), and it sparked a revolution.

Before OVA, anime creators relied on large media corporations to distribute, screen, and market their films. The companies were usually very conservative and chose to ignore experimental or controversial artists. By selling *Dallos* as an OVA, Oshii was able to bypass the corporate entities.

The success of *Dallos* was soon followed by the OVA *Fight! Iczer One*. The dark science-fiction story with a female cast had a devoted otaku following, which helped drive sales of the anime. Recognizing a profitable trend, other anime producers began selling OVAs, and by 1987 thousands of titles were available at newsstands, video stores, and markets throughout Japan.

The second technological innovation of the 1980s first appeared the same year as Oshii's OVA. In 1983 the first computer-generated images (CGI) were featured in an anime. *Golgo 13: The Professional* contained a few minutes of CGI near the end of the film. The images, created on slow computers with primitive software, are crude and jerky, not much better than hand-drawn cels. However, *Golgo 13* marks the beginning of the CGI era.

With CGI technology, artists can scan a single drawing into the computer and use software programs to automatically draw the additional images needed to make the movement fluid. Computers also insure colors remain consistent from frame to frame, something that was much more difficult when cels were hand-colored by artists.

The Golden Age of Anime

In the 1980s, changes in technology and anime distribution took place alongside a blossoming of creativity that has led historians to call this era the "golden age of anime." Much of the inspiration behind the golden age is credited to Hayao Miyazaki, also known as the Walt Disney of the East.

Miyazaki, born in 1941, saw *The Tale of the White Serpent* when he was seventeen and fell in love with the heroine of the anime. He went to work as an animator at Toei in 1963 and spent the next sixteen years trying to make his own anime. Miyazaki succeeded in 1979 with the release of his first solo effort, *Lupin III: The Castle of Cagliostro*. The anime amazed renowned American director Steven Spielberg, who secured financing for a second anime, *Nausicaä of the Valley of the Winds*. This story is an environmental drama that follows the destruction of humanity after toxic fungi and giant insects envelop the earth. *Nausicaä of the Valley of the Winds* was hailed by critics as a masterpiece, and the success of the anime allowed Miyazaki to found Studio Ghibli in 1985 with long-time collaborator Isao Takahata.

In the years that followed, Studio Ghibli produced complex and challenging films that topped box-office charts in Japan. Anime such as the 1986 *Castle in the Sky* and the 1988 *Kiki's Delivery Service* won the prestigious Anime Grand Prix awards given by *Animage*, Japan's top anime and entertainment magazine.

Violent Action

The golden age of Japanese anime was fueled by baby boomer otaku strongly influenced by Miyazaki and Tezuka. By the 1980s, some of these anime fans, like Katsuhiro Ōtomo, were able to move from obsessed fans to award-winning anime producers.

Ōtomo started his career as a manga artist in 1982. His first series, *Domu*, was about a senile old man with psychic powers who terrorizes residents in a housing development. After winning a literary award for the work, Ōtomo created the twenty-two-hundred-page epic manga *Akira*, described by *Wired* contributing writer Charles C. Mann:

> *Akira* is akin to the longest, most grandiose [grand in size and scope] cyberpunk novel ever written, a baroque tale of psychotic teens with telekinetic powers running amok in postapocalyptic Tokyo. Beneath the violent action, though, is a scary meditation on whether our increasingly powerful technology is driving us insane. Told through Otomo's elegantly detailed black-and-white drawings, *Akira* is arguably the most influential manga ever written.[40]

The groundbreaking *Akira* manga was so original that Ōtomo was able to pull together eight of Japan's largest entertainment and media companies to produce an epic anime based on the story. While most anime is produced as cheaply as possible, Ōtomo spared no expense. He created detailed

Neo-Tokyo is about to E • X • P • L • O • D • E

AKIRA

Based on the Graphic Novel by KATSUHIRO OTOMO

Art Director TOSHIHARU MIZUTANI • Chief Animator TAKASHI NAKAMURA •
Scenario IZO HASHIMOTO • Music SHOJI YAMASHIRO • Producer RYOHEI SUZUKI
Character Design / Script / Direction KATSUHIRO OTOMO

Released by STREAMLINE PICTURES   © 1989 AKIRA COMMITTEE

Akira was the number one box office hit of 1988.

scenes with more than 160,000 individual cels that made character movement beautiful and flowing.

Ōtomo's attention to detail did not come cheaply. At the time, the $11 million price tag for the production made *Akira* the costliest anime to date. The expense paid off when *Akira* became the number one Japanese box office success of 1988.

When *Akira* was released in the United States and Europe in 1989, it was a critical and cult hit, and it is credited with starting the anime boom in the West.

Anime Controversy

During the 1990s, the anime boom continued even as one of the most profitable and popular anime caused widespread controversy. In 1995 Hideaki Anno wrote and directed *Neon Genesis Evangelion*. The plot of the mecha anime would be familiar to any manga fan. A fourteen-year-old boy becomes the pilot of a monstrous biomechanical weapon called Evangelion. However, as Richmond writes, "the execution [of the story] is anything but standard, with angst, trauma, abuse, and despair galloping though the proceedings."[41]

The twenty-six episodes of *Neon Genesis Evangelion* aired on Japanese TV in 1995 and 1996, but the series was plagued with problems. The production company, Studio Gainax, ran out of funding during the eighteenth episode. With less money for artwork, the story line came to rely on extreme sex and violence. This attracted viewers, but critics said that the anime was not suitable for children.

There was little funding for Gainax to finish the last two episodes of *Evangelion*. In desperation, Anno created montages of static arty images that were meant to illustrate the thoughts of various characters. This came at the expense of the plot, which became so convoluted and confusing that many had trouble following the story line. The series ended with the story unresolved, and some fans were so troubled by this turn of events that Anno received death threats.

Evangelion in the Twenty-First Century

Despite its troubles, *Evangelion* attracted a large otaku following, which kept the series alive. In 1997 Gainax created two feature-length films, *Death & Rebirth* and *End of Evangelion*. Another film, *Revival of Evangelion*, followed in 1998. In 2003 Gainax released the entire series on DVD, called the *Renewal Project*. The shows were remastered with surround sound and CGI technology, which eliminated the jerky character movements and rendered backgrounds with more detail and color. Anime journalist Dani Cavallaro explains the importance of the *Renewal Project*: "New life was thus imbued into a chapter of anime history that had already yielded a global fandom phenomenon of unprecedented magnitude and vigor."[42]

With fans requesting even more *Evangelion*, Anno worked to satisfy demand. In 2007 Gainax began the *Rebuild of Evangelion* project. This consisted of a series of four animated films that remade the original anime series providing new scenes, settings, and characters. The first anime, *Evangelion: 1.0 You Are (Not) Alone*, was released in 2007. The plot of the first film closely resembled the first six episodes of the original low-budget TV series, but new scenes were added.

Tourists visit the pavilion of *Evangelion*. *Evangelion* generated a 144-page catalog of related products in addition to the films and DVDs.

In the late 1990s, technological developments drove new innovations in anime. With the introduction of DVDs, old anime favorites and new titles were made available for release. Unlike the VHS tapes of old, digital DVDs had many new features. Scripts were dubbed in multiple languages along with the original Japanese. In addition, anime DVDs were sold "uncut," which meant they featured scenes that were deleted or censored in the original broadcast.

Internet broadband connections also became widespread in the late 1990s. This allowed for direct streaming of anime through video-sharing websites. Broadband connections also meant amateur anime producers could show their work to a worldwide audience. By the early years of the twenty-first century, award-winning short anime such as *Genius Party* and *First Squad: The Moment of Truth* were available to viewers on YouTube and other sites.

In addition to the films and DVDs, *Evangelion* generated a 144-page catalog of related products, including cards, posters, toys, school uniforms, bags, caps, ties, gloves, key chains, pins, watches, wallets, soap, towels, umbrellas, wedding cake statuettes, video games, and over seventy-five action figures. By 2010, the financial problems previously experienced by Studio Gainax were a distant memory as the total profits for *Neon Genesis Evangelion* totaled $1.7 billion.

Fantasy Worlds

While it is one of the most successful anime, *Evangelion* is among hundreds of animated films produced every year in Japan. Some attract a few thousand otaku. Other series, like *Doraemon*, become national institutions that generate fashion trends, musical plays, video games, and countless other products.

Although technology has changed the look of anime, modern fans are attracted to the same thing that made *The Mighty Atom* a hit in 1963. Static characters from the pages of manga are given a new life as they jump, run, and fly across the screen. Anime characters entice devotees to lose themselves in a fantasy world where anything is possible and anyone can become a villain, superhero, mecha robot, or a blue-and-white cat that loves red bean pancakes.

6

Amerimanga and Americanime

In the 1960s, cartoons such as *Astro Boy*, *Speed Racer*, and *Gigantor* first appeared on American television screens. While the shows were popular, most viewers were unaware that they were watching anime created from extremely popular Japanese manga. At that time in the United States, American-made comic books like *Green Lantern*, *Superman*, *The Flash*, and *Batman* reigned supreme among teenagers. The full-color magazines had thirty-two pages, and each story concluded at the end of the issue. American comic books were nothing like Japanese manga, which were thick, black and white, and filled with stories that continued for months, or even years, before concluding.

Japanese manga remained virtually unknown in the West until the mid-1980s when *Voltron: Defender of the Universe* ran on American TV. *Voltron* was about a team of five young pilots commanding robot lions that could be combined to form the crime-fighting Voltron Lion Force. The series was pieced together from two popular Japanese anime, *Beast King GoLion* and *Armored Fleet Dairugger XV*. In order to appeal to American children, violent scenes and Japanese cultural references were removed. In addition, the script was dubbed in English, that is, the Japanese sound track was removed and replaced by one created by American voice actors.

The First Amerimanga

Voltron was an immediate ratings hit in the United States. In the years that followed, *Voltron* traveled back and forth between the United States and Japan in various forms. The American *Voltron* anime was published as a manga series in Japan. This manga was then translated into English and sold in the United States as a comic book. Finally, in 1998, an anime sequel to the original cartoon, *Voltron: The Third Dimension*, was made with CGI technology and released in Japan and the United States

In the 1980s, the Japanese *Voltron* comic book was translated into English and sold in the United States. Today, that comic is recognized as the first Amerimanga, although the

Voltron was published as a manga series in Japan before being translated into English and sold as a comic book in the United States.

word was not used at the time. In 1993 the term *American manga*, or *Amerimanga*, came into use to identify Japanese manga, like *Voltron*, that was published in English and sold in the United States. Amerimanga is also used to label manga written in English by Americans. This type of Amerimanga can be referred to as original English-language manga, or OEL. These terms are not used in Japan, however, where the government coined a different term. According to the Foreign Affairs Ministry, any manga not made in Japan is called international manga. The ministry says international manga are based on the "form of presentation and expression,"[43] or the artistic style of Japanese manga. These manga might be created in North America, Europe, China, Korea, or anywhere else in the world.

Americanime is anime made in Japan in which the Japanese dialogue has been dubbed in English. Americanime is also used to describe American-made anime that is based on the Japanese style. Whatever terms are used, Amerimanga is the fastest-growing segment of the comic business, and Americanime has been responsible for many major TV and theatrical hits.

Amerimanga from Viz

While Amerimanga is popular today, it took many years for Americans to develop a taste for comics with epic story lines and reversed pages that read from right to left. Perhaps this foreign style would never have caught on if it were not for the persistence of a single person, Seiji Horibuchi, who moved from Japan to California in 1975 and began promoting manga ten years later.

Horibuchi was not a manga fan until he read Katsuhiro Ōtomo's *Domu: A Child's Dream* in 1985. Not long after reading the story about children who possess super psychic powers, Horibuchi met Masahiro Ohga, president of Japan's largest media company, Shogakukan Inc. The company had been publishing popular manga such as *Shōnen Sunday* since the late 1950s but was not distributing manga in the United States. In an interview with the *San Francisco Examiner*,

Horibuchi tells his story: "I began talking to him about how the states lacked a major provider of Japanese pop culture. Most Japanese entertainment culture in America dealt with samurai or horror films. I wanted to start something different."[44]

Horibuchi convinced Ohga to invest two hundred thousand dollars to launch Viz Media in 1986. Within a year, the company released its first manga, an English-language version of the samurai action title *Lone Wolf and Cub*. In order to attract an American audience, Viz printed the pages "flopped" so they read from left to right. This was an extremely difficult process in the days before modern scanners and high-powered computers, but the work paid off. In 1987, *Lone Wolf and Cub* sold one hundred thousand copies in the United States. This was a considerable achievement at the time, but the sales figures of *Lone Wolf and Cub* paled in comparison to that year's most popular American comic, *X-Men*, which was selling four hundred thousand copies each month.

Gritty and Adult Pop Culture

Despite the success of *Lone Wolf and Cub*, overall manga sales in the United States languished. This situation changed in the early 1990s, when the first low-budget Japanese videos reached U.S. video stores. Many of these OVAs featured graphic sex and violence well beyond anything typically seen in American-made comics or cartoons. The explicit Japanese style was particularly appealing to older teens and people in their twenties. The video version of Ōtomo's apocalyptic cyberpunk epic *Akira* was especially popular. Former Viz editor Jason Thompson explains the impact: "Suddenly, Japanese pop culture was seen as gritty and adult. . . . In America, 'manga' became a buzzword that conjured up images of postnuclear dystopias, kinetic violence, bizarre sex, mutants, cyborgs, [and] horny tentacle beasts."[45] To capitalize on this trend, Ōtomo's twenty-two-hundred-page *Akira* manga was translated and published in English as Amerimanga.

COSPLAY

In 1984, Japanese studio head Nobuyuki Takahashi attended a science-fiction convention in Los Angeles. He was amazed when he saw hundreds of people dressed up as their favorite characters from Japanese science-fiction manga. To describe the activity, Takahashi coined the term *cosplay,* short for *costume role-playing*. Since that time, cosplay has become a favorite activity of dedicated fans of manga and anime.

In Japan, otaku teenagers gather on weekends in Tokyo's Akihabara district, where dozens of cosplay cafés have opened for dedicated anime and manga fans. In the United States, the cosplay trend was ignited in the late 1990s when girls began to dress up as their favorite *Sailor Moon* characters. Today, thousands who attend comic and anime conventions in the United States engage in cosplay. With dozens of conventions held in cities across the country every year, the opportunity to dress up as a manga superhero is no longer restricted to Halloween.

The *Akira* series was popular among the loyal fan base, but it took a group of magical girls to create an American pop culture sensation. In 1996 the *Sailor Moon* anime series began running on the USA cable network. The blonde superhero Sailor Moon and her Sailor Soldiers soon found a dedicated audience of American female fans. Within a year, teenage girls were attending comic book conventions, or comic-cons, dressed as their favorite *Sailor Moon* magical girls. This activity, known as "cosplay," or costume role-playing, is very popular in Japan, where male and female otaku dress up as manga and anime characters on a regular basis.

A year after *Sailor Moon* appeared on television, a New York publication called *MixxZine* ran the serialized manga translated into English. *MixxZine* was a new publication, one of the first in the United States to have the look and feel of a dense, Japanese-style "telephone book" manga. The cover was in color, and the inner pages were inexpensive newsprint, the type of paper used for newspapers. *MixxZine* was, in the words of its cofounder Stuart Levy, "thick and cheap."[46] Each magazine featured four manga series. Two series were ultraviolent shōnen manga called *Ice Blade* and *Parasyte*. The other two were shōjo series, *Magic Knight Rayearth* and *Sailor Moon*. In Japan, shōnen and shōjo are never featured together in a single issue, because it is assumed that boys would not be interested in girls' comics and that girls would not be interested in boys' stories. Levy knew it was risky to run these opposing styles in one publication but says he believed fans would buy *MixxZine* for their favorite series and then "discover the appeal of different manga styles."[47]

Dressing up as manga and anime characters, or cosplay, became popular at comic book conventions in the United States and around the world.

In 1970 comic book fan Shel Dorf organized the first comic book convention in San Diego, called the Golden State Comic-Con. Dorf was surprised when over three hundred fans turned up to talk about their favorite characters, meet with artists, and swap comic books. In 1973 the event was renamed San Diego Comic-Con, and interest in the convention has been steadily growing. In 2009 the three-day event attracted over 126,000 people, and thousands were turned away from the sold-out event.

Americanime and Amerimanga have been part of Comic-Con since the late 1980s. In 2010 the newest anime titles were screened for tens of thousands of fans, and mangaka from Japan held popular seminars. Moto Hagio, the renowned pioneer of shōjo manga, was featured at a question-and-answer panel. Other panel discussion included The Best and Worst of Manga of 2010, Robotech: The First Quarter Century, and Viz Media's *Vampire Knight*. Comic-Con is also visited by major movie stars, such as Angelina Jolie, Bruce Willis, Eva Mendes, and Samuel L. Jackson, who attend the event to promote their films.

In 2009 the San Diego Comic-Con attracted over 126,000 people.

Unflopped *Dragon Ball Z*

The *Sailor Moon* anime series achieved astounding widespread popularity in 1998, when the anime began running on the Cartoon Network. That year, Viz began publishing another manga series destined to make an impact on American culture. *Dragon Ball Z*, aimed at preteen boys, was created by Akira Toriyama and ran in Japan between 1985 and 1995. *Dragon Ball Z* follows the exploits of a monkey-tailed alien raised by a kung fu master on earth.

Toriyama was initially reluctant to let Viz publish *Dragon Ball Z* in 1998. He was unhappy about the flopped versions of his manga that had previously appeared in the United States. The artist complained that the characters seemed to be left-handed and the scenes did not look right. This prompted Viz to publish *Dragon Ball Z* in what Thompson calls "unflopped,"[48] or in the original right-to-left, sequence.

In 2001 when the *Dragon Ball Z* anime began appearing on the Cartoon Network, sales of the unflopped Amerimanga took off. Some readers were initially confused by the Japanese style, but others considered it a badge of honor to read the manga in its true format. Whatever the case, *Dragon Ball Z* ranks among the most successful Amerimanga and Americanime in history.

Scanlation

The success of *Dragon Ball Z* created thousands of new fans for Amerimanga. Viz released a number of unflopped titles, but the publisher had trouble keeping up with demand. This inspired a few Americans to take matters into their own hands. In 2001 a bilingual manga fan called AC of Troy, who spoke English and Japanese, started a website called Toriyama's World to publish digital versions of Akira Toriyama's manga that were unavailable in American stores.

AC of Troy pioneered the process now known as scanlation. He obtained Toriyama manga by purchasing the printed volumes over the Internet. Using a scanner to digitize the work, AC of Troy translated the manga into English and posted the pages online. Scanlation violates copyright laws because it is done without permission from artists. A copyright gives artists, writers, and publishers the right to control how their original works are published. Despite the questionable legality of scanlation, Toriyama's World was one of the few places English-speaking manga fans could read their favorite titles. The first day it was online, Toriyama's World received ten hits, but within a few years the site was attracting over 10 million users a day.

The success of Toriyama's World required AC of Troy and a small staff to work incredibly long hours to scan and translate thousands of manga pages. The number of postings slowed after a time, and fans drifted to new sites launched to imitate Toriyama's World. By 2009 the original scanlation site had shut down.

Unfiltered Manga

In 2001, just as Toriyama's World was starting up, Stuart Levy founded Tokyopop to publish and distribute Amerimanga. Tokyopop created its first series of Amerimanga in a paperback book form called graphic novels in April 2002. The graphic novels were sold at mall bookstores like Borders and Waldenbooks. Tokyopop marketed the books as "unfiltered" because they were unflopped.

At the time, the average mall bookstore only sold fifteen or twenty graphic novel titles. Most stores refused to carry books with the unflopped format. This soon changed as the Tokyopop titles attracted a significant audience. Some bookstores, such as Waldenbooks, set up entire sections filled with Amerimanga, and sales soared. In 2002 Amerimanga generated about $20 million, about one-third of total graphic novel sales. By 2006 Amerimanga sales were two-thirds of the graphic novel industry, and total graphic novel sales climbed to $330 million.

Shōjo OEL

Some of the most popular Amerimanga graphic novels are shōjo manga series such as *Paradise Kiss*, *Peach Girl*, and

Princess Knight. The appearance of these titles inspired a new generation of American female mangaka to create original English-language manga. While women make up only a small percentage of OEL creators, they quickly gained notice in an industry dominated by men. The artist Rivkah, creator of the OEL series *Steady Beat*, comments on the female mangaka phenomenon: "I think [women are] the future of manga. I get a lot of e-mails from fans who say, 'I never read manga until I started reading your comics, because I can relate to the characters.' Which is fine with me."[49]

Steady Beat, published by Tokyopop, tells the story of two sisters who grow up in a conservative Christian household. Drama ensues when the older sister announces she is a lesbian. Lillian Diaz-Przybyl, Rivkah's editor at Tokyopop, explains why OEL manga such as *Steady Beat* are popular with American readers: "As much as I adore Japanese manga, there is something about it which many American readers find limiting. Rivkah has [a very good grasp of the] shojo style, but she's telling a story set in Austin [Texas], a pretty realistic depiction of what it's like . . . in the U.S."[50]

Despite the fact that American mangaka can create more relevant stories for English-speaking readers, OEL remains less than 20 percent of Tokyopop's market. Of the four hundred titles the company publishes every year, only about seventy are OEL. About fifteen of these series are created by female mangaka.

The Afro Samurai Fusion

American and Japanese mangaka operate in separate worlds with little collaboration. This is not the case with animators, as Richmond writes: "The creative relationship between the two countries has become so intertwined that for some projects it's difficult to pinpoint on which side of the Pacific the initial inspiration comes from."[51] This is certainly true of *Afro Samurai*, about a character named Afro who is a wandering samurai living in the future. Afro is obsessed with tracking down and killing his father's murderer.

JAPANESE MANGA TO AMERICAN ANIME

Producer Eric Calderon describes the difficulty of turning the Japanese manga Afro Samurai *into an Americanime:*

[*A*ll] of the dialogue had to be changed because it's written in Japanese and then it comes back as really horrible Janglish [Japanese/English gibberish]. When a character says, "I am for you finding the ultimate goal, that is which I will be number one, for [also] the power of the world I will have like God." I say, "Yeah, we'll probably have to work on that." There were other things . . . I would try to maintain the expectation that people wanted us to be [tough] all the time. [So] because of that we didn't really want to see a drifting Japanese samurai story for three episodes. We wanted people to be fighting every couple of minutes. We wanted Afro to be really [tough]. We didn't want him to make long speeches about how he really misses his father.

Quoted in Daniel Robert Epstein. "Afro Samurai: Eric Calderon Interview." UGO Entertainment. www.ugo.com/ugo/html/article/?id=16498.

Afro Samurai started out in 1999 as a Japanese seinen manga series written and illustrated by Takashi Okazaki. The manga, inspired by Okazaki's love of soul and hip-hop music, was self-published in very limited editions. Although only four thousand copies of *Afro Samurai* existed, the manga was discovered by Eric Calderon, a former MTV animation executive working for Gonzo Studio in Japan. Calderon describes his cross-cultural role at Gonzo:

They hired me to try to create fusion Japanese animation which is Japanese animation that is made in collaboration with western talent or western companies in order to make something that is more marketable for the world rather than just the Japanese market. . . .

[What] I saw in *Afro Samurai* was a very Japanese samurai story but with this freestyle element and a western influence that would bring that idea to the American audience.[52]

Calderon worked with American actor Samuel L. Jackson, who expressed great interest in *Afro Samurai*. Jackson's celebrity star power helped turn *Afro Samurai* into a cross-Pacific project. Japanese illustrators at Gonzo create a five-episode anime. Jackson provided the voice of Afro, and the musical score was created by American hip-hop artist RZA from the rap group Wu-Tang Clan. The original creator, Okazaki, also collaborated on the project.

Samuel L. Jackson (left) with creator Takashi Okazai, provided the voice of Afro in the anime *Afro Samurai: Resurrection*.

Afro Samurai premiered on Spike TV in English with Japanese subtitles and was released in 2007 on television in Japan, dubbed into Japanese. All five episodes were also released on iTunes.

Korean Anime

Afro Samurai is only one example of the cross-cultural influences found in international anime. South Korea is the world's third-largest producer of anime, after the United States and Japan. Despite the popularity of the Japanese art style, South Korea's relationship with Japan is complicated.

Japan annexed Korea in 1910 and ruled the nation until the end of World War II in 1945. Because of anti-Japanese feelings, anime was banned in Korea until 1998. Producers skirted the ban by dubbing Japanese anime into Korean. Scenes depicting Japan and Japanese culture were deleted.

Sometimes Koreans simply remade Japanese anime. For example, the Korean show *Robot Taekwon V* is a close copy of *Mazinger Z*. However, not all Korean animation is imitation. Original anime, such as *Yobi, the Five Tailed Fox*, based on Korean folktales, is very popular throughout Asia. In addition, South Korean animators have collaborated with Americans for years, producing popular TV shows such as *The Simpsons* and *Family Guy*.

Koreans produce their own style of manga, called manhwa, published in the United States by Tokyopop. Manhwa characters generally have exaggerated facial features but realistically proportioned bodies. Unlike manga, the books read left to right, which makes them more accessible to Americans. Some of the most popular Tokyopop manhwa titles include the action fantasy series *King of Hell* and a Gothic vampire tale called *Model*.

International Manga Awards

Manga has become an international phenomenon since the late 1990s. While non-Japanese mangaka long labored in obscurity, in recent years they have been able to gain worldwide recognition through the International Manga Awards. The award program was originally started in 2007 by Japan's minister of foreign affairs, Taro Aso, to encourage the creation of international mangaka. Aso, who became prime minister in 2008, is popularly known as Rozen Aso because of his love for the Goth manga *Rozen Maiden*.

The scope of the International Manga Awards demonstrates how far Japanese manga has come since the 1950s. In

Japanese foreign minister Taro Aso (left) awards artist Lee Chi Ching (right) the "Nobel Prize of Manga."

2008, judges for the International Manga Awards received 146 entries from 26 countries, including China, France, Australia, Malaysia, Russia, and Thailand. Commenting on the spread of manga to several dozen countries, Thompson writes, "What 20 years ago seemed too culturally specific for export has become another extension of Japan's . . . gross national cool."[53]

In the 2010s, some American manga otaku are learning Japanese in order to read manga before it is translated. It is uncertain if Mickey Mouse and Donald Duck will be replaced by Doraemon or Afro Samurai anytime soon. But with dedicated scanlators, translators, publishers, and otaku on both sides of the Pacific, there is little doubt manga and anime characters will continue to mix and mingle on the international scene. The worldwide impact of the ancient Japanese artistic style cannot be denied and will continue to amaze and amuse for many years to come.

Notes

Introduction: Whimsical Pictures

1. Douglas McGray. "Japan's Gross National Cool." *Foreign Policy*, June/July 2002, p. 45.
2. Jocelyn Bouqillard and Christophe Bouquillard. *Hokusai: The First Manga Master*. New York: Abrams, 2007, p. 9.
3. Daniel Pink. "Japan Ink: Inside the Manga Industrial Complex." *Wired*, October 27, 2007. www.wired.com/techbiz/media/magazine/15-11/ff_manga?currentPage=1.
4. Quoted in Martin Webb. "Manga by Any Other Name Is . . ." *Japan Times Online*. May 28, 2006. http://search.japantimes.co.jp/cgi-bin/fl20060528x1.html.

Chapter 1: Roots of Manga

5. Frederik L. Schodt. "Manga, Japanese Comics & Graphic Novels." History of Art. www.all-art.org/art_20th_century/manga/m001.html.
6. Frederik L. Schodt. *Manga! Manga! The World of Japanese Comics*. Tokyo: Kodansha, 1997, pp. 28–29.
7. Schodt. *Manga! Manga!* p. 30.
8. Quoted in John Stevens and Alice Rae Yelen. *Zenga: Brushstrokes of Enlightenment*. New Orleans: New Orleans Museum of Art, 1990, p. 14.
9. Quoted in Stephen Addiss. *Zenga and Nanga*. New Orleans: New Orleans Museum of Art, 1976, p. 82.
10. Stevens and Yelen. *Zenga*, p. 14.
11. Sheri Le. "Manga: Evolution." The Right Stuff, June 10, 2010. www.rightstuf.com/rssite/main/anime Resources/2002/evolution.

Chapter 2: Manga Emerges

12. Schodt. *Manga! Manga!* p. 38.
13. Quoted in Coulton Waugh. *The Comics*. New York: Macmillan, 1991, p. 6.
14. Quoted in Schodt. *Manga! Manga!* p. 43.
15. Helen McCarthy. *The Art of Osamu Tezuka*. New York: Abrams Comic Arts, 2009, p. 27.
16. Quoted in McCarthy. *The Art of Osamu Tezuka*, p. 81.
17. Quoted in Aaron H. Bynum. "Interview with Fred Schodt." Animation Insider, September 19, 2007.

Chapter 3: Shōnen Manga

18. Quoted in Mark W. MacWilliams, ed. *Japanese Visual Culture*. Armonk, NY: East Gate, 2008, p. 38.
19. Paul Gravett. *Manga: Sixty Years of Japanese Comics*. New York: Harper Design International, 2004, p. 56.
20. Quoted in Deb Aoki. "Interview: Yoshihiro Tatsumi." About.com. http://manga.about.com/od/mangaartist interviews/a/YTatsumi.htm.
21. Quoted in Aoki. "Interview."
22. Quoted in Frederik L. Schodt. *The Astro Boy Essays*. Berkeley, CA: Stone Bridge, 2007, p. 109.
23. Quoted in Sherif Awad. "Education Through Animation." Egypt Today, December 2009. www.egypttoday.com/article.aspx?ArticleID=8741.
24. Gravett. *Manga*, p. 59.

Chapter 4: The Girls' World of Shōjo Manga

25. Quoted in Schodt. *Manga! Manga!* p. 97.
26. Schodt. *Manga! Manga!* p. 98.
27. Gravett. *Manga*, p. 79.
28. Quoted in MacWilliams. *Japanese Visual Culture*, pp. 123–24.
29. Quoted in MacWilliams. *Japanese Visual Culture*, p. 125.
30. Schodt. *Manga! Manga!* p. 101.
31. Deb Aoki. "Top 10 Shojo Manga Must-Reads." About.com. http://manga.about.com/od/recommendedread ing/tp/top10shojo.htm.
32. Deb Aoki. "Top 10 Shojo Manga Must-Reads."

Chapter 5: Anime

33. Quoted in "Japan Appoints Cartoon Ambassador." MSNBC, March 19, 2008. www.msnbc.msn.com/id/23716592.
34. Quoted in "Japan Appoints Cartoon Ambassador." MSNBC.
35. Simon Richmond. *The Rough Guide to Anime*. London: Rough Guides, 2009, p. v.
36. McCarthy. *The Art of Osamu Tezuka*, p. 151.
37. Richmond. *The Rough Guide to Anime*, p. 12.
38. Quoted in Osamu Tezuka. *Astro Boy*, vol. 1. Milwaukie, OR: Dark Horse, 2002, p. 1.
39. Quoted in Margaret O'Connell. "Why Is Manga and Anime Characters' Hair All the Colors of the Rainbow? Part 3: Blonds Are Trouble." Sequential Tart, April 2004. www.sequentialtart.com/archive/apr04/cv_0404_2.shtml.
40. Charles C. Mann. "The Giants of Anime Are Coming." *Wired*, September 2004. www.wired.com/wired/archive/12.09/anime.html?pg=4&topic=anime&topic_set=.
41. Richmond. *The Rough Guide to Anime*, p. 90.
42. Dani Cavallaro. *The Art of Studio Gainax*. Jefferson, NC: McFarland, 2009, p. 60.

Chapter 6: Amerimanga and Americanime

43. Quoted in "Amerimanga." Serving History. www.servinghistory.com/topics/amerimanga.
44. Quoted in Will Reisman. "Seiji Horibuchi: Japanese Culture on U.S. Shores." *Examiner*, January 21, 2008. www.examiner.com/a-1170543~Seiji_Horibuchi_Japanese_culture_on_U_S__shores.html.
45. Jason Thompson. "How Manga Conquered the U.S., a Graphic Guide to Japan's Coolest Export." *Wired*, October 23, 2007. www.wired.com/special_multimedia/2007/1511_ff_manga.
46. Quoted in Adam Arnold. "Full Circle: The Unofficial History of Mixx-Zine." *Anime Fringe*, June 2000. www.animefringe.com/magazine/00.06/feature/1/index.php3.
47. Quoted in Arnold. "Full Circle."
48. Thompson. "How Manga Conquered the U.S., a Graphic Guide to Japan's Coolest Export."
49. Quoted in Jeff Salamon. "Manga, American-Style." Tokyopop, April 23, 2007. www.tokyopop.com/Robofish/insidetp/688417.html.
50. Quoted in Salamon. "Manga, American-Style."
51. Richmond. *The Rough Guide to Anime*, p. 236.
52. Quoted in Daniel Robert Epstein. "Afro Samurai: Eric Calderon Interview." UGO Entertainment. www.ugo.com/ugo/html/article/?id=16498, 2010.
53. Thompson. "How Manga Conquered the U.S., a Graphic Guide to Japan's Coolest Export."

Glossary

Americanime: Japanese anime dubbed in English or English-language anime produced in the Japanese style.

Amerimanga: Japanese manga sold in North America, with the text translated into English.

anime: Animated cartoons made in Japan.

dub: To replace the original language in a film with a different language; for example, when the dialogue in a Japanese anime is replaced with English.

gekiga: Literally "drama pictures," the term is used to describe serious, dramatic adult manga that reflects the grim realities of life in a dark, starkly realistic, and violent manner.

josei manga: This style, which translates as "ladies manga," was created for housewives and young clerical workers from ages eighteen to thirty-five.

manga: Japanese comics.

mangaka: A person or persons who create manga stories and illustrations.

otaku: A person or persons with an obsessive interest in manga, anime, video games, or computers.

seinen: Literally "young man," this term is used to describe manga created for at an eighteen- to thirty-year-old male audience, with some aimed at businessmen well into their forties.

shōjo manga: Literally "girls' comics," aimed at female audiences between the ages of eight and eighteen.

shōnen manga: Literally "comics for boys," written primarily for males ages eight to eighteen.

Books

Tite Kubo. *Bleach*. vol. 1. San Francisco: Viz Media, 2008. The first volume of the best-selling and beloved Amerimanga that helped spawn a merchandising phenomenon that includes TV and feature-length anime, CDs, video games, and rock musicals.

John Layman and David Hutchison. *The Complete Idiot's Guide to Drawing Manga Illustrated*. 2nd ed. Indianapolis: Alpha, 2008. Covers the fundamentals of drawing various manga characters, landscapes, and environments, with instruction on storytelling methods. This book features step-by-step illustrations that guide readers from the basic strokes to the final ink renderings.

Helen McCarthy. *The Art of Osamu Tezuka*. New York: Abrams ComicArts, 2009. Written by a leading authority on Japanese animation and comics, this oversized book is filled with beautiful color pictures of Tezuka's work through the decades and includes a DVD of the artist at work in his cramped Tokyo studio in the late 1970s.

Simon Richmond. *The Rough Guide to Anime*. London: Rough Guides, 2009. An introduction to the world of Japanese anime, with stories behind award-winning productions, a list of fifty must-see pictures, and details on the most influential artists and directors.

Frederik L. Schodt. *Manga! Manga! The World of Japanese Comics*. Tokyo: Kodansha, 1997. Although this book is dated, it is the manga "bible" responsible for introducing a generation of Americans to Japanese manga. The author is the ultimate manga insider, who worked closely with Osamu Tezuka for years and was the first to translate his work into English.

Megumi Tachikawa. *Otacool—Worldwide Otaku Rooms*. Tokyo: Kotobukiya, 2009. Photographs of bedrooms and other rooms created by fanatical manga and anime fans, with close-ups of the creators and the action figures, posters, clothing, furniture, appliances, and other knickknacks collected by otaku enthusiasts.

Websites

Animation World Network (www.awn.com). The latest news about animation and anime, merchandise, blogs, and events. The anime section features the latest theatrical and DVD releases and videos by directors, artists, and other creators.

"Manga," About.com (http://manga.about.com). This site, hosted by Deb Aoki, a published cartoonist and former art teacher, offers the latest manga and Japanese pop culture news, photos, news from manga conventions, interviews with artists, and articles about the history of manga.

Manga Jouhou (www.manganews.net). This is a scanlation information site with the latest manga news, blogs, links to Japanese and American publishers, and scanned pages of popular manga series. The site also contains self-published work from amateur mangaka.

Index

A

Abiko, Moto (Fujiko Fujio), 69, *70*
AC of Troy, 93, 94
Afro-Samurai (manga/anime series), 95–98
Akira (manga series), 80–82, *81*, 89–90
American manga (Amerimanga), 10
  Dragon Ball Z and popularity of, 93
  early, 87–88
  growth in sales of, 94
  shōjo OEL genre, 94–95
  from Viz media, 88–89
Animal Scrolls, 14, 16
Animation
  creation of, 74, 76
  first, 71
  See also Original video animation
Anime, 71
  golden age of, 79–80
  Korean, 98
Anno, Hideaki, 82
ASIMO (robot), 47, *47*
Aso, Taro, 99, *99*
Astro Boy, 38–40, *39*
Astro Boy (cartoon series), 39, 74, 76, 86

B

Bleach (manga series), 53
Bringing Up Father (comic strip), 32–33, *33*
Buddhism, 13, 15
  cosmology of, 16–17

C

Calderon, Eric, 96–97
Caricature (fushi), 14
Comics, American, manga *vs.*, 10
The Complete Manga Works of Tezuka Osamu, 41
Cosplay (costume role-playing), 90, *91*

D

Dainan Gate, *22*
Dallos (anime), 77–79
Diary of Ma-chen (comic strip), 35–36
Disney, Walt, 71, 73
Domu: A Child's Dream (Otomo), 88
Doraemon (cartoon robot), 69–70, 72
Dorf, Shel, 92
Dororo (manga series), 52–53
Dragon Ball Z (manga series), 93

E

Easy-Going Daddy (comic strip), 33–34
Evangelion (mecha anime series), 82–84

F

Fabulous Forty-Niners, 57
Felix the Cat (comic strip), 32
Fight! Iczer One (anime), 79
Floating world (ukiyo), 20–22
Fruits Basket (shōjo manga series), 67–68
Fujimoto, Hiroshi, 69, 70
Fujio, Fujiko. *See* Abiko, Moto

G
Gautama, Siddhartha, 15
Geisha, 21
Gekiga (drawing style), 46
Global manga, 10–11
Golgo 13: The Professional, 78, *78*, 79
Good Bye (Tatsumi), 46
Gravett, Paul, 44–45, 54, 60

H
Hagio, Moto, 57, 92
Hakuin, Ekaku, 18
Hearst, William Randolph, 30
The Heart of Thomas (Hagio), 57
Hell (Tatsumi), 46, 48
Hell Scrolls, 16, 17
Hino, Matsuri, 66, 67
Hogan's Alley (cartoon strip), 30, 31
Hokusai, Katsushika, 8, 9, 22–23
Homosexuality, 58–59
Honey and Clover (josei manga series), 64
Horibuchi, Seiji, 88–89
Hungry Ghost Scrolls, 17

I
Ikeda, Riyoko, 57–58
International Manga Awards, 98–100
Iron Man #28 (Tetsujin 28-gō), 49, *49,*
   49–51

J
Jackson, Samuel L., 97, *97*
Japan
   opening of international trade with, 23,
   25
   U.S. occupation of, 35
Japan Punch (magazine), 28–29
Josei manga, 63–64, 68

K
Kamakura period, 16
Kami (spirits), 72
Kamio, Yoko, 68

Kanji (ideograms), 14
Katō, Ken'ichi, 42
Kitayama, Seitarō, 71
Kitazawa, Rakuten, 30, 32
Komura, Masahiko, 69
Kubo, Tite, 53

L
Lee Chi Ching, *99*
Levy, Stuart, 94
Lone Wolf and Cub (manga), 89
Lost World (Tezuka), 36
Lupin III: The Castle of Cagliostro
   (anime), 79

M
MacArthur, Douglas, 35
Magnificent 24s (*Showa 24*), 57–58,
   60, 68
Manga
   American influences on, 30, 32–33
   flopped *vs.* unflopped formats, 93
   international, 88
   meaning of, 8–9
   as propaganda, 34–35
   supernatural stories in, 52–53
   taboo subjects in, 57–59
   See also specific types
Manga Shōnen (magazine), 42–43
Manhwa (Korean manga), 98
Mazinger Z (mecha manga), 51
Mecha/mecha manga, 47, 49, 51–52
Meiji (Japanese emperor), *24,* 25
Mighty Atom (Tetsuwan Atomu),
   38
The Mighty Atom (anime TV
   program), 47, 73–74, *75,* 76
Miuchi, Suzue, 68
MixxZine (magazine), 90–91
Miyazaki, Hayao, 79, 80
Momotarō (amine), 71
Monet, Claude, 25
The Monkey and the Crab (amine), 71

N

Nagai, Go, 44, 51

Nakayoshi (*Best Friend,* magazine), 65

Nausicaä of the Valley of the Winds (anime), 79–80

Neon Genesis Evangelion (mecha anime), 82, 84

New Treasure Island (Tezuka), 36

New York Journal (newspaper), 30, 31

New York World (newspaper), 30

Ninja, 46

O

OEL (original English-language) manga, 94–95

Ohga, Masahiro, 88, 89

Okazai, Takashi, *97*

Okmoto, Ippei, 32

Original English-language (OEL) manga, 94–95

Original video animation (OVA), 78–79

Osamu Tezuka Manga Museum, 41

Oshii, Mamoru, 77

Ōtomo, Katsuhiro, 80–81, 88, 89

Otsu-e (paintings), 18–19, 20

Outcault, R.F., 31

P

Panda and the Magic Serpent (amine), 71

Perry, Matthew C., 23, 25

Pin-Pin Sei-Cha (comic strip), 36

The Poe Family (Hagio), 57

Portrait of Pia (Satonaka), 55

Pretty Soldier Sailor Moon (Takeuchi), 64, 66

Princess Knight (shojo anime), 77

Princess Mononoke, 72, *72*

Pulitzer, Joseph, 30

R

Rivkah, 95

Robots, 47, 69-70, 72

  mecha and, 48–50

Robot Taekwon V (Korean anime), 98

RZA, 97

S

Sailor Moon (anime series), 65, *65,* 90

Samurai manga, 45

Samurai warriors, 19

San Diego Comic-Con, 92, *92*

Satonaka, Machiko, 55–56, 60

Satori (enlightenment), 17

Scanlation, 93–94

School of Manga (Kyoto Seika University), 59

Sengai, Gibon, 18

Shōjo Friend (manga magazine), 56–57

Shōjo manga (girls' comics), 55–57, *61*

  artistic style of, 60–63

  magical girl genre, 66

  taboo subjects broached by, 57–59

  themes of, 59–60

Shōnen Club (magazine), 34, 35

Shōnen Jump (magazine), 44, 54

Shōnen manga, 42-43, 54

  female characters in, 50

Shunga (spring pictures), 21–22

Steady Beat (OEL manga series), 95

T

Tagosaku and Mokube Sightseeing in Tokyo (comic strip), 32

Takahashi, Rumiko, 62

Takaya, Natsuki, *67*

Takemiya, Keiko, 59

Takeuchi, Naoko, 64

The Tale of the White Serpent (amine), 71, 79

Tatsumi, Yoshihiro, 46, 48

Tezuka, Osamu, 35, 36–37, 38, 39, 40–41, 74

  anime work of, 73–74, 76

  on drawing, 40

  supernatural comics of, 52–53

They Were Eleven (Hagio), 57

Thirty Six Views of Mount Fuji (Hokusai), 9
Toba (Buddhist priest), 14, 16, 23
Tokyopop, 94
Tokyo Punch (magazine), 32
Tomorrow Will Shine (Satonaka), 60
To My Respected Elder Brother (Ikeda), 57–58
Toriyama's World (website), 93, 94
The Transformers (TV program), 51–52, *52*

U
Ukiyo-e (floating world pictures), 21
Umino, Chica, 64
Urusei Yatsura (manga series), 62

V
The Vampire Knight (shōjo manga series), 67
Voltron (manga series), 86–88

W
Walt Disney Studios, 71, 74, 76
Weekly Shōnen Jump (manga magazine), 44, 53
Western art, first influence of Japanese art on, 25–26
Wirgman, Charles, 28–29
Women
  as characters in shōnen manga, 50
  as manga artists, 57, 95
World War II, 34–35

Y
Yellow Kid, 31, *31*
Yokoyama, Mitsuteru, 49
Yoritomo (warrior chief), 19

Z
Zen Buddhism, 15, 17–18
Zenga (religious cartooning), 17–18

Picture Credits

About the Author

Stuart A. Kallen is the author of more than 250 nonfiction books for children and young adults. He has written on topics ranging from the theory of relativity to the history of rock and roll. In addition, Kallen has written award-winning children's videos and television scripts. In his spare time, he is a singer/songwriter/guitarist in San Diego.